A Magna Field Guide

MUSHROOMS

A Magna Field Guide
MUSHROOMS

By Mirko Svrček

Illustrated by Bohumil Vančura

MAGNA BOOKS

Text by Mirko Svrček
Translated by Daniela Coxon
Illustrated by Bohumil Vančura
Graphic design by Soňa Valoušková

This English edition published 1994 by
Harveys Bookshop Ltd.,
Magna Road, Wingston, Leicester LE8 2ZH,
and produced in co-operation with
Arcturus Publishing Limited

© 1990 Aventinum, Prague
First published 1975 by Artia, Prague

ISBN 1-85422-778-5
Printed in the Czech Republic
3/10/11/51-05

CONTENTS

FOREWORD

Man has been a mushroom fancier for a very long time. His attention must first have been attracted to them by the unusual shape of their fruit-bodies, which suddenly appear after rain in striking quantities in fields and woodlands. Similarly their gay colouring, short life span and finally their edible and poisonous attributes were and are distinguishing features. As botanical knowledge increased, mushrooms became the subject of serious study. They were recognized as the simplest of organisms and so very different from others, that they were regarded as the lowest form of plant life. Unfortunately the botanists' concern with mushrooms was until recently only slight, if it existed at all. Mycology only developed into an independent scientific discipline due to research in the second half of the 19th century and today it represents an extensive field of knowledge. The study implications of mycology extend into a number of other areas, for example, phytopathology, which involves the study of diseases. The pharmaceutical and food industries also derive benefit from such know-ledge. The main aim of this book, however, is to provide some basic information about the nature of mushrooms and to stimulate a further and deeper interest in their study.

The choice of illustrated species has been limited to the larger fungi, which represent a very important section of the extensive and total fungus population. Nevertheless, the introductory chapters also include that large group of microscopic fungi, which an ordinary mushroom-picker would probably fail to identify.

The study and collection of mushrooms can be an interesting pastime and because it requires active movement in the fresh air, it often becomes a sporting passion which can be continuously satisfying and mentally relaxing. A serious study of mycology should be supported by a sound knowledge of the other biological sciences, especially botany. A know-ledge of plants, of their habitats and above all of those of woodlands, which are directly associated with fungi, furthers an understanding of the problems of their existence. The colour plates, therefore, illustrate the relationship between the chosen fungi and their most common environment.

7

WHAT ARE FUNGI?

The term fungus does not only encompass the large, often colourful and striking fruit-bodies of the fleshy, edible or poisonous mushrooms found in woods, but it also incorporates a large group of inconspicuous microscopic organisms, such as moulds and yeast-fungi. They all share several common characteristics which differentiate them from plants and animals and which transform them into an independent plant kingdom with distinctive shapes and behavioural patterns. These also play an important part in the transformation of matter and the earth's life cycle.

Fungi are organisms which lack the chlorophyll pigment, whose fruit-bodies are usually filamentous and composed of minute tubes called *hyphae*. They reproduce by spores, both through sexual and asexual generation. Because fungi contain no chlorophyll, they are not able to produce independently the complex organic substances such as sugar, fat and starch. Therefore they absorb their organic nourishment in an already digested form from other living or dead organisms. This type of nutritional feeding is called heterotrophic and it resembles the animal method of nourishment.

Other characteristics of fungi are, however, reminiscent of the vegetable kingdom. The way which they originated is not as yet fully understood. So far the most reasonable theory, accepted by the majority of scientists, maintains that they shared a common ancestor with protozoa and that at an early stage of evolution they became separated and as a subsequent independent group they went through a complex process of development. Their history is undoubtedly a very long one, but because their soft fruit-bodies are never preserved as fossils, their prehistoric traces are very rare occurrences. The oldest findings date back to the Palaeozoic (Devonian) era of approximately 350 million years ago. The exact number of familiar fungus species which have been identified up to this point in time cannot be accurately stated, as the description of the range of genera and species varies considerably from one expert to another. The number of fungi currently listed greatly exceeds 100,000 species, but because many of these names are synonymic, the figure should be reduced to about 60,000; but this, of course, increases every year with the discovery of new species.

The discipline which deals with the study of fungi is called mycology. Its importance is growing, due to further basic research in this field. Its influence extends into many other economically important pursuits, such as production of food, pharmacology and medicine.

THE STRUCTURE AND SHAPE
OF THE FUNGUS FRUIT-BODY

The part which is picked and which is misleadingly called a mushroom, is in fact only the fruit-body of a larger fungus. The scientific term used to describe the main body or thallus of a fungus is *mycelium*. This is a mass of delicate filaments called hyphae which are often invisible to the human eye. These hyphae can penetrate various types of material ranging from a woodland humus and rotting wood to the tissues of living plants. In some fungi the mycelium develops into a mass of thin or thick roots, threads or even thick cords. The mycelium obtains nutrients from decomposing organic matter. Some types of fungi grow on their mycelium hardened, tuberous, globular or irregular formations, which have a dark surface. They are called *sclerotia* and store reserves of food and enable such fungi to survive even in unfavourable growing conditions. In some types of fungi, these sclerotia can later develop into fruit-bodies.

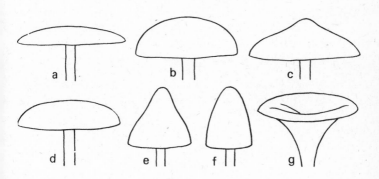

Fig. 1. Various types of cap in Gill fungi: a — expanded, b — semiglobulate, c — conical with umbo, d — broadly convex, e — bell-shaped, f — conical, g — funnel-shaped.

The life of mycelia varies considerably; some last one to two years, others for several years. The mycelia of mycorrhizal fungi, which live in symbiosis with the roots of green plants, usually last as long as the host plants.

The mycelia of other fungi, such as the Fairy-ring champignon *(Marasmius oreades)* or Blewits *(Lepista saeva)*, spread evenly in all directions over the ground so that after a number of years they form very large circles, whose fruit-bodies start to develop at certain times during the year. At ground level it may be difficult to see that they do in fact form a circle at all.

Aerial photography on the other hand often reveals these old fungus circles very clearly because of the darker colour of the grass at the edge of the circle. These circles are sometimes popularly thought to have magical qualities and are known as fairy rings. However, the most distinctive mycelium is that of the Honey fungus *(Armillaria mellea)*, which grows thick, dark-coloured, branched rhizomorphs rather like bootlaces covered by a shiny, hard skin.

Out of the mycelium grow the fruit-bodies. These are constructed of densely interwoven hyphae and, according to the type of fungus, they adopt a variety of shapes. The study and differentiation of these systems of hyphal tissue are important criteria in the recognition of the mutual affinity of fungi as well as in their classification. The size of fruit-bodies varies from

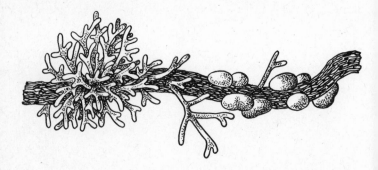

Fig. 2. Coralloid and tubercular mycorrhizae on the roots of the Scots pine *(Pinus silvestris)*.

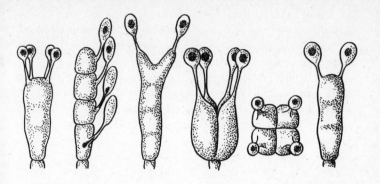

Fig. 3. Various types of fertile, terminal, basidia cells with their spores.

microscopic micron measurements to several tens of centimetres. Fruit-bodies also contain the reproductive organs. The range of their common features, covering shape, colouring and size, is a constant factor in every systematic group (order, family and genus), but individual characteristics often vary considerably. In this respect the microscopic features of fungi are the most reliable.

The growth of fruit-bodies is influenced by internal and external preconditions and the rate of growth differs from one species to another. The fruit-bodies of Ink Caps (*Coprinus* species) develop very quickly indeed, taking only a few hours to reach maturity, but they do not survive for very long and soon dis-

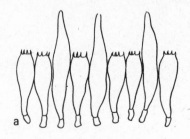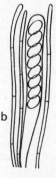

Fig. 4. a — Basidiomycete with basidia and cystidia; b — Ascomycete with ascus and paraphyses.

13

appear. Slow-growing species include the fruit-bodies of the Polyporaceae family, which are perennial species. Their fruit-bodies produce annually one additional fertile layer and it is not unknown for some of these fungi to live for scores of years.

The fruit-bodies of higher fungi, which are the main subject of this book, consist usually of a stipe and a cap. The stipe is cylindrical and its apex is crowned by the characteristically widened cap. Its underside *(hymenophore)* assumes different forms according to the particular species. In Gill fungi and Boleti (Agaricales) it consists of gills or tubes, while in Tooth fungi (Hydnaceae) the lower surface of the cap is covered with teeth or spines. The underside is covered by a fertile layer *(hymenium)* of spore-bearing projections, called *basidia*, which produce spores. In the Cup fungus this fertile layer forms the inner lining of the cup, whereas in such fungi as the Morels and the Staghorn fungus it covers the whole or part of the outside of the irregular fruit-body. In the Puff-balls the spores are produced in great quantity inside the fruit-body and finally escape when it opens through a pore at the top or falls to pieces.

The young fruit-bodies of Gill fungi and Boleti (Agaricales) are globular or ovate in shape and are often entirely covered by an external skin known as a universal veil. As the fruit-body

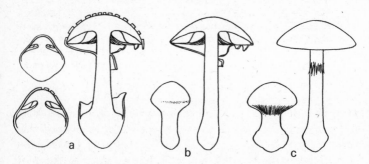

Fig. 5. Schematic development of the volva, ring, warts and cortina on the fruit-bodies of Gill fungi: a — development of the volva at the base of the stipe and of the warts on the cap surface, which derive from the universal veil; b — development of the ring; c — development of the cortina.

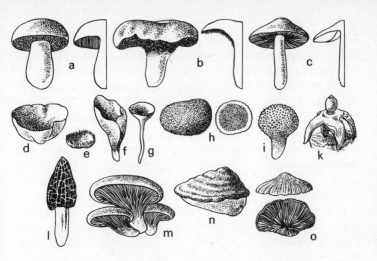

Fig. 6. Various types of fruit-bodies: a — fruit-body of the Boletales showing cap, stipe and tubes (a longitudinal cross-section of half of the fruit-body); b— fruit-body of the Hydnaceae with spines on the underside of the cap; c — fruit-body of Gill fungus with gills on the underside of the cap; d-h — fruit-bodies of the Discomycetes; d — deeply cup-shaped fruit-body *(Peziza)*; e — shallow, cup-shaped fruit-body with fringed edge; f — the straightening process of an ear-shaped fruit-body which is open on one side; g — cup-shaped fruit-body with a long stipe; h — fruit-body of a Morel *(Morchella)*; i — tuberous fruit-body of an Elaphomyces; k — fruit-body of a Puff-ball *(Lycoperdon)*; l — fruit-body of an Earth-star *(Geastrum)*; m — fruit-body of the Oyster mushroom *(Pleurotus ostreatus)*; n — fruit-body of a polypore *(Fomes;* hoof-shaped, attached behind); o — fan-shaped fruit-body (the Split-Gill — *Schizophyllum commune)*.

grows and develops, this veil bursts open leaving scales both on the cap and the stipe. This sort of veil is typical of fungi that belong to the *Amanita* genus. In the Death Cap *(A. phalloides)* the lower part, shaped like a cup, is left standing at the base of the stipe and is known as the volva. In some species it forms a membranous edging, or rings, which hang from the extended stipe, while its upper part forms warts or patches on the cap. In other types the veil is only partial, joining the edge of the

15

cup to the stipe while the fruit-body is young and leaving one or several rings half way up the stipe, after it ruptures.

The veil can be membranous, fibrous or slimy. In the *Cortinarius* genus it is cobweb-like as it stretches between the edge of the growing cap and the stipe and is called the cortina. However, it often does not develop fully and is noticeable only on the young fruit-bodies, whilst later it disappears altogether. The *Amanita* genus has both the universal and partial veil, in other fungus species the veil is barely noticeable.

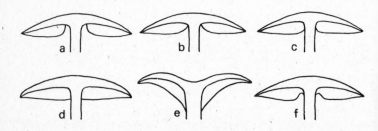

Fig. 7. Various types of gill attachment to the stipe: a — remote; b— free; c — adnexed; d — adnate; e — decurrent; f — sinuate.

REPRODUCTION OF FUNGI

The reproduction of fungi is a complicated process. As previously mentioned, it can be both sexual and asexual. Asexual reproduction generally occurs through the disintegration of the mycelium into individual cells, which each form new independent mycelia. On other occasions such individual cells detach themselves from the ends of fertile hyphal tubes and then develop into new mycelia. Sexual reproduction, however, is very complicated indeed and can take place in a number of ways.

Finally, in some types of fungi sexual and asexual reproduction alternate in the two phases, which make up the life cycle of such fungi.

By way of illustration, one method of reproduction of the higher fungi will be dealt with as this applies to the majority of those fungi which can be picked and are edible. The mycelium,

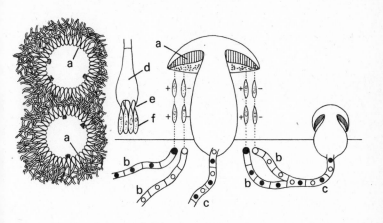

Fig. 8. Propagation of fungi: a — hymenium, b — primary mycelium, c — secondary mycelium, d — basidia, e — sterigma, f — spore.

which is the proper body of these fungi, forms fruit-bodies under favourable conditions. They are usually equipped with a cap, which constitutes their reproductive organ and can be compared to a poppy seed head in terms of the similarity in function. The fertile cells *(basidia)*, from which the spores detach themselves, form a spore-bearing layer called the *hymenium*. This covers the gills and fills the inside walls of the tubular depressions, which are located on the underside of the fungus caps. Each of the basidia usually forms four spores, which become detached as they ripen. These spores have the same shape but their physiology differs, two being male spores and two female. Under favourable conditions these spores grow into primary mycelia which are, however, not yet capable of producing fruit-bodies. These can only develop from the secondary mycelia, which result from the fusion of male and female primary mycelia, and the whole cycle is then repeated.

In many instances, the number of spores produced by one fruit-body is extremely high. For example one fruit-body of *Polyporus squamosus* can produce many million spores, whilst *Langermannia gigantea*, which often measures up to 50 cm in diameter, produces several billions or trillions of them. Despite this high fertility only a small number of spores actually give rise to new fruit-bodies.

CLASSIFICATION OF FUNGI

Like other organisms, fungi can also be classified according to certain features and characteristics into various taxonomic groups.

Ascomycetes represent the largest of all fungus classes. Their number is estimated at about 30,000 species. Their distinguishing features are spores, which are held in an embracing membrane or sac, known as *ascus*. Their classification is based on the structure of their fruit-bodies, on their evolution and shape and also on the shape of their sacs and spores. Larger and more conspicuous fruit-bodies are only found in some of the Discomycetes, such as Morels, False Morels, True Cup fungi and Truffles. These fruit-bodies are shaped like cups, discs or tubers and they either cling to the ground or grow on a stipe.

On the other hand Basidiomycetes is the most highly developed class of fungi. Their spores are produced in basidia. The shape of their fruit-bodies varies a great deal and this group includes about 90 % of all fungi which can be found in woodlands. Their total number is estimated at 15,000 species. The largest and most important of these are divided into two groups: Hymenomycetes and Gasteromycetes. The first group is characterized by its hymenium, which is almost permanently open, prior to the ripening of its spores. The hymenium in the second group is always closed and only opens when the spores have ripened.

THE LIFE CYCLE OF FUNGI

Fungi either obtain their nourishment in a parasitic manner from living organisms or else they are saprophytes feeding off dead and decomposing matter. A characteristic feature of many fungi is the symbiotic association of their mycelia with the roots of seed plants. This association is called mycorrhiza and is beneficial to both partners. For example all Boletus species, as well as other fungi, live in symbiosis with trees and therefore certain species of mushrooms can be found under certain types of trees. Saprophytic fungi have mycelia that absorb water containing dissolved minerals, which are the products of organic breakdown and decay. This group includes the majority of fungi which can be found in woods growing on such materials as soil, humus, fallen leaves and needles, dead wood, tree stumps and trunks. In contrast parasitic fungi attack living organisms and penetrate their system, and by absorbing their food supplies

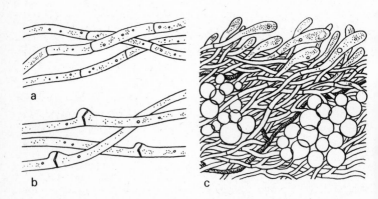

Fig. 9. Hyphae: a — septate without clamp connections; b — septate with clamp connections; c — example of fruit-body structure of a *Russula* showing various types of cells.

they damage, weaken and finally destroy them completely. The largest number of these parasites are microscopic fungi. The most harmful of the large parasitic fungi are some Polypores (Polyporaceae), Honey fungus *(Armillaria mellea)*, *Pholiota* and *Pleurotus*. The grouping of parasitic and saprophytic fungi has not been strictly defined and there is a number of fungi which can exist both on living or dead trees.

Since the fruit-bodies of fungi are made up of as much as 95% water, a plentiful supply of it is a basic precondition of their growth. As for temperature requirements, some fungi develop their fruit-bodies only in low temperatures, while others, which include the majority of fungi found in Europe, need rather warm conditions. The radiation of the sun is not an absolute pre-requisite and is only marginally required for the formation of fruit-bodies. However, fungi growing for example in mines do not often produce developed fruit-bodies or if they do they are usually deformed as a result of the absence of sunlight.

Fungi are very common and their omnipresence is due to their ability to grow in almost any type of material. According to their ecological requirements, which are often of a very specific and closely defined nature, fungi can be divided into several groups. One of them includes the fungi which always grow in areas devastated by fire, especially in coniferous forests, such as *Pholiota carbonaria*, *Tephrocybe carbonaria*, the Ink Cap *(Coprinus boudieri)* and some Cup fungi *(Geopyxis carbonaria* and *Rhizina undulata)*. A number of fungi can be found living on the excrements of herbivorous animals and on manure heaps and the state of decomposition determines the type of fungi that will grow in it. They range from proper moulds *(Phycomycetes)* to Gill fungi *(Agaricales)*, which also include the impressive Ink Cap *(Coprinus* species*)*. Sometimes fungi even grow as parasites on other fungi, but this phenomenon is quite rare, and only in some regions does *Boletus parasiticus* grow in large numbers on the fruit-bodies of Earth-balls *(Scleroderma* species). Finally some fungi even attack insects, especially their caterpillars and pupae, as in the case of *Cordyceps militaris*.

DISTRIBUTION OF FUNGI

Fungi are more widely distributed than green plants. The degree of the proliferation of individual species is dependent upon their ecological requirements, on climate (temperature and humidity) and on the presence of the appropriate soil or host plant. Although the microscopic spores can be carried by the wind to remote areas, it is improbable that the special conditions necessary for the life and reproduction of those fungi are fulfilled in such places.

Nevertheless fungi growing in the temperate zones of the northern hemisphere are closely related and the majority of species are common to all European countries. However, the existence of some fungi can be narrowly confined to one particular type of soil in a given habitat. In addition, there are a large number of fungi which to date have only been found in one locality and are unknown elsewhere. North America is very rich in fungi and only about one third of its species are common to Europe. Generally, the areas rich in vegetation, especially woodlands, also have a plentiful supply of fungi. The temperate zone is rich in saprophytic fungi, which are dependent on woodland humus and a high rainfall, and also in wood fungi, which are most numerous in the habitats undisturbed by man, such as virgin forests and natural reservations. In southern regions the number of saprophytic and woodland fungi steadily decreases and their incidence is restricted to mountainous areas. On the other hand, parasitic fungi are more numerous here and their numbers are largest in the tropics.

Some species are cosmopolitan and, providing that they have basic living conditions, they may be found over practically the entire surface of the earth. For example *Schizophyllum commune* grows on various trees extending from the polar regions to the tropics. Similarly the Fly Agaric *(Amanita muscaria)* and *Collybia dryophila* can be found in almost any woodland area in Scandinavia, Siberia and Canada, all over Europe and as far as North Africa. On the other hand, *Amanita caesarea*, which is a warmth-loving species, is limited to a smaller area, which in the northern hemisphere is approximately synonymous with the vine-growing areas.

Altitude does not influence the growth of fungi as much as it does that of green plants. Fungi in fact grow in the mountains alongside other vegetation. These include some remarkable mountain species which do not exist at lower altitudes or are generally rare, but thrive in certain microclimatic conditions (e.g. in deep, damp river valleys).

As already mentioned, the occurrence of fungi is closely related to the distribution of green plants, whose existence is paralleled by fungi over the entire surface of the earth. Parasitic fungi are naturally more dependent on living plants then fungi living on decaying organic matter and humus or directly upon seemingly barren soil. However, the close dependence of such species on certain vegetable communities is soon evident, although in some conditions fungi are even capable of creating their own independent communities. Certain species are often associated either with woodland vegetation or that of steppes or meadowland. The differences in the distribution pattern can be studied by comparing the mycoflora of alder thickets, peat-bogs or oak and hornbeam groves, with fungi which occur in sandy pine forests or mountain beech woods and spruce plantations. The selection by individual fungus species of a given geographical region and a specific community of plants and animals in a certain area is called biocenosis. It is also influenced by the geology of the area, by the mineral composition of its soil and by its average rainfall.

THE IMPORTANCE OF FUNGI FOR MAN

Fungi play an important role in terms of ecology. They include a number of species which can have a directly harmful effect on mankind as they are poisonous or can cause skin and other diseases. Other species damage our society indirectly by causing economic losses through parasitic attacks on important vegetation. Many microscopic species, on the other hand, provide an invaluable service for man, for instance in the fermentation industry. These fungi, producing certain chemical substances (enzymes) which ferment sugar into alcohol and carbon dioxide, have been used in the production of a range of alcoholic drinks for a very long time. Fermentation is caused by certain bacteria, yeast fungi and moulds. In the past, the process of fermentation was allowed to take its natural course. However, the resultant liquid often contained micro-organisms, which caused secondary fermentation (e.g. lactic and acetic) as well as other chemical reactions, which gave the final product an unpleasant taste, smell and colour. Today only pure cultures of a single micro-organism are employed. This industry is dependent on the microscopic fermenting fungi, of which the most important are yeast-fungi. They include *Saccharomyces cerevisiae*, which is grown in pure cultures and is all-important for the brewing industry. Pure, brewing yeast-fungi are also used in bread-making for the necessary fermentation. Other species of yeast-fungi are used in wine-making to ferment fruit juices, in the milk industry for the production of various fermented milk products. Apart from bacteria, an important role is played by moulds from the *Penicillium* genus in the ripening of some cheeses, such as Roquefort and Gorgonzola, in which the mould grows inside the cheese and forms a network of greyish veins. In Camembert these veins only cover the surface area. However, the most revolutionary discovery was that of antibiotics made from fungi, in particular that of penicillin, which was isolated from *Penicillium notatum* and which nowadays successfully cures a number of infectious diseases.

Fungi play an active part in natural decomposition and in this way they indirectly influence many fields of human activity. The decay of organic matter is caused by the joint activity of bacteria and fungi, particularly microscopic fungi, which are to be found everywhere in the soil in large numbers. In fact every type of soil, whether it comes from woodlands or fields, is saturated with the spores and hyphae of these organisms. Soil fungi perform an important mechanical role in that they store carbon dioxide and cause various chemical reactions. They participate in the breakdown of vegetable matter, in the creation of compost, in the various methods of fodder conservation and in the treatment of some agricultural products. Finally water fungi partially contribute to the self-purification process of polluted waters.

Setting aside such positive and beneficial attributes, fungi can also prove to be very dangerous enemies and no matter how hard man fights against them, it is an uneven contest. The potential harm caused by fungi can be illustrated in a number of ways; for example parasitic fungi attack economically valuable plants and animals and even man himself. Fungi parasitizing on man can cause various skin diseases and even general disorders. They can provoke diseases of the respiratory system and auditory passage if their spores penetrate the blood stream. These diseases are common to both man and animals. In particular fish are susceptible to water moulds, which settle on damaged skin tissue and gradually spread throughout the organism. Other moulds which attack insects are used as insecticides.

Tremendous damage is caused by fungi parasitizing on economically important plants, as they decrease plant yield or make it impossible to cultivate some plants in certain areas. These fungi are the concern of that branch of scientific study called phytopathology, which deals with plant diseases. This important science studies not only the causes, development and course of plant diseases, but it also endeavours to develop methods which would prevent, confine or cure such diseases.

Apart from bacteria, viruses and insects, most damage is caused by microscopic fungi, such as rust, blight and mould. These moulds lead to a general wasting of seedlings and also precipitate dangerous diseases in potato plants and vines. Blight specifically attacks wheat and some dust blight can destroy whole ears of corn and transform them into a mass of black spores; on the other hand, hard blight leaves corn ears alone. Similarly large losses in wheat production have been caused by wheat rust, whilst various types of rust attack other plant species with little regard to their economic importance. Especially harmful is mildew, which forms a white floury film on many plants, such as hops, roses, oak trees and vines. Fruit is also attacked by fungi which cause black or brown rot. Other species damage the needles of coniferous trees and ultimately make them drop off. *Claviceps purpurea* is a notorious pest, which also attacks wheat and rye but at the same time provides a vital source of important drugs necessary in the pharmaceutical industry. Wood fungi, mainly members of the Polyporales order, are also very dangerous; their mycelia penetrate the wood of trees and eventually destroy them. There are also other species which attack trees, the commonest being the Honey fungus *(Armillaria mellea)*, which is one of the most harmful parasites that predominantly infests both forest and garden trees. Another fungus which is greatly feared is *Serpula lacrymans*, which engenders serious dry rot in buildings and thrives on rising dampness in their badly ventilated lower parts and on the static, damp air in such places. Such wood fungi have been known to attack wooden frameworks and supports in mines with attendant great losses of men and materials.

This chapter naturally cannot cover all the knowledge which has been accumulated about fungi and their relationship with man and his activities, but, mention must be made of the important place that fungi occupy in our nutrition. Edible mushrooms can be picked in woods and they are also grown commercially. The most important of these are Field mushrooms, whose popularity has grown in recent years; also there are Oyster fungi *(Pleurotus ostreatus)*, *Stropharia rugoso-annulata*, and *Boletus edulis* which in some countries have important economic value. As a result of their unknown qualities, fungi have also become an important object of research with beneficial results in the fields of cytology, genetics, physiology and biochemistry.

As can be seen, the importance of fungi touches upon a number of fields of human activity and it is often greater than we might imagine. Due to their omnipresence and extensive numbers fungi play an important role in the life cycle of the earth.

MUSHROOM PICKING
AND THEIR IDENTIFICATION

Mushroom picking has become a favourite pastime in many countries. However, as the number of mushroom-pickers has greatly increased, some mushroom species are becoming very rare, especially in the vicinity of large cities and it is by no means as easy to find them in such great quantities now as it used to be. The knowledge of experienced mushroom-pickers is usually fortuitous, but a real study of the life cycle of fungi can be of great assistance and successfully deepens such accidental and episodic information. Such academic knowledge leads the mushroom-picker to certain types of trees, which provide the necessary conditions for certain fungus species; similarly it helps him to plan his expeditions according to the weather, as for instance during protracted droughts fungi grow better in the damper parts of woods. Again, dense forests on the leeward side of mountains have sufficient sunshine, a rich, dark humus and an extensive variety of tree species and as a result usually abound in fungi. On the other hand, a plethora of a single kind of fungus can often be found in woodland monocultures. For example, mossy, sloping spruce forests provide a likely habitat for *Boletus edulis* and the Chantarelle *(Cantharellus cibarius)*, whereas the grassy banks around ponds with associated oak trees play host to *Boletus reticulatus* and birch and aspen woods are a suitable habitat for *Boletus scaber* and *B. aurantiacus*. In late autumn many fruit-bodies of *Boletus badius, Tricholoma flavovirens* and *T. portentosum* can be found growing in sandy, pine forests, whilst Field mushrooms, also called Champignons *(Agaricus campestris)*, as well as Fairy-ring champignons *(Marasmius oreades)* grow in fertilized meadows and pastures.

When picking mushrooms it is advisable to respect the peaceful woodland atmosphere. Mushrooms can either be cut off or pulled out. The most suitable receptacle for their collection is a wicker basket or a box, in which mushrooms cannot be damaged. When the mushroom is picked, its stipe at least should be cleaned straight away. Another time-honoured rule is that only quite familiar species should be collected for food. Other, as yet unknown species can be identified with the help of suitable literature, but it is always better to consult a mycologist or an experienced mushroom-picker for additional advice in order to avoid unpleasant repercussions. Fungi exhibitions and field study expeditions organized by experts can also help the public to recognize different varieties of fungi.

The identification of fungi is a very difficult and complicated task for the beginner. In recognizing mushrooms it is not possible to rely merely on a colour illustration of the specimen. Even specialized literature contains only a small number of really valuable illustrations which provide an accurate colour guide and also record the seasonal variations in colour, which are often considerable and make the identification of species very difficult indeed for an unexperienced collector. Moreover, beginners fail to appreciate the often subtle yet characteristic features of individual species which differentiate them from other, quite similar fungi. For an accurate identification of a fungus a close comparison with the detailed description in the text is much more important and decisive than that in the accompanying supplementary illustration, which provides only a visual image of the species. Luckily, there are a number of fungi which are so specific in appearance that it is possible to recognize them at first sight. These species form the majority of fungi described in this book.

FUNGI UNDER THE MICROSCOPE

It is not the objective of this book to supply directions for the serious scientific study of fungi. If the interest in mycology is deeper, further information may be obtained from the recommended specialized literature and also from a professional mycologist who will supply the fundamental framework of knowledge, which is the prerequisite for such a study. This also requires a good microscope and basic laboratory equipment, which for beginners can be very simple. It should include materials needed for microscopic research and the preparations of microscopic specimens — such chemicals as Melzer's reagent and green vitriol. Because the fruit-bodies of fleshy fungi do not last long, it is essential to prepare detailed specimen descriptions from fresh material. Such descriptions should contain details of shape, measurements, colouring, smell, textural colour changes along with the data about the locality of the find and its general habitat and finally the date and name of the collector. The fungus should be either photographed or sketched and only then can it be dried out. Finally the dried specimens can then be collected in a herbarium. Every specimen should be kept in a separate envelope accompanied by the data generally associated with all botanical collections. Only collections maintained in this way have any real scientific value.

If a microscope is available, sections of fungoid fruit-bodies should be occasionally prepared to observe the remarkable textures of these organisms. Similarly, fungus spores offer an interesting and colourful picture. Their size ranges from 5 to 10 microns; they can be colourless or coloured in the shades of pink, yellow, brown or blackish; their shape is usually elliptical; their body wall can be either thin or thick, smooth or ornamented, i.e. covered with small protruberances, spines or ridges. Perhaps their most distinctive feature, however, is amyloidity or the blue-staining of the spore and hyphal walls,

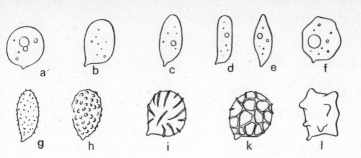

Fig. 10. Various spore-shapes: a — globular, b — oval, c — ellipsoid, d — cylindrical, e — fusoid, f — angular, g to l — spores with various ornamentation, g — echinulate, h — warted, i — ridged, k — reticulate, l — nodulose.

which can be highlighted by a chemical reaction using Melzer's reagent. This feature is a permanent characteristic of some species and even of larger groups of fungi belonging to the Basidiomycetes. The spores ejected from the hymenium form a powder, which is white, brown, yellow, pink or black in colour and which serves as an established and critical characteristic for the purposes of classification. This can be easily discovered by putting a cap that has been freshly detached from the fruit-body on white paper with its gills facing downwards and then leaving it under a bowl or a glass or even inside a plastic bag. After a few hours the ripe spores will start to fall on to the paper. Another distinguishing feature is the character of the hymenium, or fertile layer of the fungus fruit-body. In the microstudy of fungi an important role is also played by the structure of the cuticle of the cap, which consists of long filaments or globular cells. The anatomical structure of the gills *(trama)* is also important. Basically it can be one of the four following types: irregular, regular, bilateral and inverse. The nature of the gill flesh can be accurately established by taking thin, transverse slices with a razor blade.

EDIBLE MUSHROOMS

The value of fungi for man largely stems from the existence of edible mushrooms, for the fruit-bodies of some species have traditionally been consumed throughout the ages. The number of species identified as edible in the past remained very small for a long time without increasing. This was perhaps due to the fact that edible mushrooms usually grow in the same localities as almost identical poisonous fungi and therefore their lack of popularity often belied their quality. The Romans, who were renowned for their epicureanism, regarded some mushrooms as excellent food. They gave pride of place to *Amanita caesarea*, which they called 'boletus' and which was served at every imperial banquet. Its excellent taste even captured the attention of poets who composed epigrams and eulogies in praise of this mushroom. The Romans also liked Boleti, which they called *suillus*, and Truffles called *tuber*. The information found in the writings of such early natural scientists as Pliny and Galen shows that other, less common and tasty mushrooms were also eaten.

Many centuries elapsed and the views of the majority of people vis à vis the value of certain edible species still remained quite conservative, particularly in some European countries. However, the number and popularity of edible species have subsequently increased in some countries, where picking mushrooms has become a sport and a hobby and sometimes even a time-consuming passion. Whilst it is true that the number of poisonous species is very small in comparison with the edible or harmless ones, it is also true that edible mushrooms are not all of the same high quality. Species producing only small fruit-bodies, which lack substance, have little culinary potential. The economically important species are those common edible mushrooms which have a pleasant taste, produce large fleshy fruit-bodies and usually grow in large numbers in a particular place.

All non-poisonous fungi can be divided into edible and inedible species. The line drawn between these groups is not accurately defined and is often determined subjectively according to personal taste and inclination. However, the number of mushroom species which can be sold on the open market is dependent on official approval and recognition. In Europe, this number amounts to about 70 edible species. These include all the good edible mushrooms which .grow in European forests; all can be freely sold with the exception of *Russula* species, which can be confused with some poisonous species and as a result it has been deemed inadvisable to allow them to be offered for sale.

Some of these edible mushrooms can be cultivated with success. The best known are Truffles, which are grown in oak forests on a calcareous soil in the warm regions of southern France. Other mushrooms whose popularity has increased during the last few decades are Field mushrooms. Cultivation of the latter has been started in countries which used to import them in the past. Further recent developments in the field of mushroom growing include the successful promotion of the Oyster fungus *(Pleurotus ostreatus)* in Hungary and *Stropharia rugosoannulata* in East Germany. Finally, certain other mushrooms can be grown in smaller quantities, for example such wood fungi as *Kuehneromyces mutabilis*, *Pleurotus cornucopiae* and *Flammulina velutipes*. To do this, dead wood in the shape of a stump or a part of a tree trunk which has become infested with the mycelia of the above-mentioned fungi is usually transferred to a suitable place in the garden or a cellar and kept moist by regular watering in order to maintain the fertility of the mycelia.

The decision as to which mushroom should be considered the tastiest and best for cooking is in the final analysis a question of personal choice. However, a nearly perfect mushroom flavour can be achieved by blending together several species of edible mushrooms, such as the range of Boleti and Gill fungi. Again, some mushrooms are best when pickled in vinegar, others when dried, fried or roasted. Generally the following types are considered the best of the edible species: Boleti, especially *Boletus edulis*, Champignons or the common Field mushrooms (*Agaricus* species), *Amanita rubescens*, *Calocybe gambosum*, *Tricholoma flavovi-*

rens, T. portentosum, the Parasol mushroom *(Lepiota procera)* and the Shaggy Parasol *(L. rhacodes), Lycoperdon perlatum* — although young fruit-bodies only, *Morchella, Discina,* the Chantarelle *(Cantharellus cibarius),* the Honey fungus *(Armillaria mellea),* the Oyster fungus *(Pleurotus ostreatus), Lactarius volemus,* the Fairy-ring champignon *(Marasmius oreades)* and *Lactarius deliciosus,* which is particularly suitable for pickling, and finally some edible *Russula* species.

COOKING WITH MUSHROOMS

Although mushrooms are more of a delicacy than a regular food, their nutritional value must not be under-estimated. They play a varied yet traditional role in a variety of dishes. As such they represent a supplementary food additive, which fulfils an important biological and health-protecting function. Mushrooms are usually not as rich in protein as meat and also contain some nitrogenous chemicals in a form which makes digestion difficult. Thus it is common knowledge that dishes prepared from mushrooms are difficult to digest and cannot be recommended for sick people or those who suffer from indigestion. In any case, mushrooms should not be eaten in large quantities. Primarily they serve as a supplementary item for a major dish or can be used as a condiment, as they add a characteristic flavour to various dishes and often have a very delicate taste. Dishes with mushrooms as a main ingredient, such as scrambled eggs and mushrooms, can provide an illusion of a meat course, but apart from the nourishment supplied by the eggs and fat, their protein value is negligible.

Mushrooms contain approximately the same or perhaps a slightly higher quantity of water than vegetables, and additionally salt (about 1%), sugar and rather less than 1% of fat. Nitrogenous substances form about 1.5 to 6%, but one of these constituents is practically indigestible. The largest quantity of protein is found in Field mushrooms, in Puff-balls, especially in their smaller fruit-bodies, and also in some Boletus species. Other mushrooms, such as the *Tricholoma* species, have very low protein content. Mushrooms, however, are rich in vitamins, namely vitamin A in the form of carotene, vitamins B_1 and B_2 (for nervous disorders) whilst some contain a small quantity of vitamin D. Vitamin C is generally missing or present only in very small quantities.

The general feeling is that young fruit-bodies have the greatest nutritional value. Their membranes are thin and therefore easy to digest. In older, ripe fruit-bodies the largest percentage of the most valuable minerals is located in the spores, but the human body is largely unable to benefit from them as they are covered by firm, cellular membranes. The flavour value is the most important aspect in the appreciation of mushrooms. The aromatic substances they contain give the dishes prepared of them a delicious taste. In fact, their role is similar to that of spices. It is because of this that mushrooms are often added to soups or they are even prepared as a main course with other trimmings. They are also a popular constituent of gravies, patés and stuffings.

Because mushrooms grow in large quantities for only a short period of the year, they are preserved in a number of ways. Sterilized mushrooms are preserved after heating without chemical additives; for instance in their own juice, in tomato purée, in edible fats, in wine, or pickled in salt or vinegar. The most popular and simplest way of mushroom conservation is by drying them out. The well-cleaned fruit bodies should be thinly sliced (1 to 3 mm.) and then placed on paper, a wooden board or best of all some taut netting. Mushrooms should be dried in a moderate but constant level of heat, above the stove or on central heating radiators or directly in sunshine. The best places for drying out mushrooms in summer are well-ventilated lofts. When thoroughly dried, mushrooms should be placed in airtight glass containers with wide necks in order to retain their flavour and avoid the effect of fluctuations in the dampness of the air because mushrooms are very hygroscopic. This also protects them from various insects. An age-old and more elaborate and time-consuming method of drying is by threading mushrooms on long pieces of cotton, which are then suspended above a source of heat.

The dried mushroom segments, especially the small pieces, can also be turned into powder, which is then mixed with pepper and cloves. A powder prepared in this manner is a suitable ingredient for soups and sauces.

Another possible method of preserving mushrooms is by preparing mushroom extract. This is a thickened juice obtained from fresh or dried mushrooms by steeping them. Usually old mushrooms are more suitable for making this extract because they often contain a large amount of water and so their dehydration would be a difficult and long process. After the mushrooms have been cleaned, sliced and washed, salt is added and they are then cooked in their own juice. When they start to produce juice, this is poured off and thickened by further boiling. The extract is then bottled and can also be seasoned with pepper and cloves. The bottles should be sterilized by steam beforehand and given an air-tight seal. The flavour of such an extract can be improved by the addition of vegetables such as celery, onions or parsnips. The extract should be kept in small bottles to ensure that it is consumed fairly quickly and to prevent it from being attacked by moulds, which often happens in large bottles when they are kept open for a long period of time.

However, the pickling of mushrooms in salt is often considered to be the most profitable way of retaining the unique flavour of mushrooms. Cleaned and well-drained mushrooms are cut into small pieces and put in layers, alternating with layers of salt, into wide-necked glass containers. In this respect it is very important that mushrooms are well drained, as if not they would produce too much water and thus increase the quantity of salt required in their pickling. The layers must be packed closely together and the salt solution must be concentrated. This is clearly visible when particles of salt at the bottom of the container do not dissolve. Mushrooms preserved in this way keep for a long time. During this period they can be added to a variety of dishes but only in small quantities in order to prevent oversalting.

The most popular way of preserving mushrooms in the majority of countries is pickling them in vinegar. The simplest method is as follows: cleaned and washed mushrooms, cut into large pieces or left whole in the case of small fruit-bodies, are placed in a pan which is half filled with water. After adding salt, whole peppercorns and bay leaves, this mixture is then boiled for 20 minutes. Next the mushrooms are strained, mixed with a reasonable amount of raw onion ring slices and the entire mixture is finally put into preserving jars. If preferred a half-boiled carrot, similarly sliced, can also be added. The contents are then covered by a slightly sweetened vinegar, to which has been added a teaspoonful of salt per pint and which should not be boiled. The jars are closed with air-tight lids and sterilized by boiling for half an hour. Mushrooms preserved in this fashion have an unlimited lifespan.

Another possible method of preserving is by putting the mushrooms in boiling, salty water and allowing them to boil for a short time. Then they are strained and left to drip. Meanwhile salted vinegar is boiled with several peppercorns, pimento and a bay leaf; rings of sliced onion and a carrot cut lengthwise are then added along with some sugar, the ratio being four lumps of sugar to one litre of vinegar. When the carrot is tender, the mushrooms are again added and briefly brought to the boil. After the mixture has cooled down, it is strained and the vinegar purified by straining through a linen cloth. The mushrooms are then placed in layers in glass containers, alternating with layers of carrots and onions. The jars must be filled to the top with the strained vinegar, properly sealed and finally sterilized. The best flavour can be achieved by using a mixture of several species of mushrooms.

This method of sterilization used in mushroom preservation allows for further processing in winter. Finely cut, raw fruit-bodies are pressed into preserving jars, whose lids are then sealed and the jars finally sterilized by boiling for three quarters of an hour. Such mushrooms can subsequently be used as if they were fresh. They can be sterilized in their own juice. The cleaned mushrooms are sliced, salted and (dry) steamed until tender when they still retain about a quarter of their juice; on no account must they be allowed to dry up. A quarter-litre bottle then takes about 500 g of mushrooms and with every 1 kg of mushrooms 20 g of salt and a pinch of carraway seeds should be added. When the mushrooms are cool, the preserving bottles are filled with them and sterilized for 40 minutes at a temperature of 100°C. Mushrooms sterilized in this way can be fried with eggs or added to sauces.

If the mushrooms are to be sterilized in fat, they should be first cleaned, sliced, salted and then sautéed in fat. 100 grams of boiled butter for every 400 g of mushrooms provides a sufficient quantity for a quarter-litre bottle, to which 10 to 20 g of salt is also added. The tender mushrooms are then cooled, pressed into the preserving jars, the melted butter is poured in and the mixture is finally sterilized at 100°C. Mushrooms preserved in this way can be added to sauces, stuffings, cooked with meat or served on their own.

Roasting mushrooms in salt is another lesser known method of preservation. The fruit-bodies are cleaned, thinly sliced and after mixing with salt (about a quarter of the mushroom weight), they are immediately dry cooked over a moderate heat. They should be constantly mixed and roasted until completely dry. Finally the mushrooms are placed along with the salt into bottles, which should be firmly sealed. With every method of sterilization it is advisable to cut the mushrooms into really small pieces so that the conserving agents effectively penetrate them and this forestalls any possible decay through imperfect preservation.

It has been customary in preceding mushroom manuals to warn against the consumption of reheated dishes containing mushrooms. However, in this respect mushrooms are not more sensitive than other dishes containing protein. As long as the food is stored in a cool place, best of all in a refrigerator, to prevent changes caused by bacterial activity, it remains in perfect condition, but should be eaten within 2 days.

POISONOUS MUSHROOMS AND TYPES
OF POISONING CAUSED BY THEM

The most deadly poisonous fungi are two types of Death Cap called *Amanita phalloides* and its albino form *A. phalloides* ssp. *verna*. Their caps are white or various shades of green, their cuticle does not usually exhibit any remnants of a veil whilst their stipe, which widens at the base, is encased in a tall, membranous, white volva. The stipe also has a ring and the gills are permanently white. Their fruit-bodies as well as the spores contain at least 10 poisonous substances which include phalloidin and amanitoxin. Phalloidin attacks the liver cells and acts very quickly; in fact, within 15 minutes it can cause cellular changes. A fatal dose is about 1 milligram to each kilogram of the body-weight of a human being. A perspective can be realized when it is known that 100 g of the fresh fruit-bodies of the Death Cap, or the equivalent of 5 g of dried mushrooms, contain approximately 10 mg of this poisonous substance. Appreciably more dangerous, however, is the presence of amanitoxins in such fungi, which again attack liver cells. Their lethal effect is slower and thus disguised; the first signs of poisoning only appear after 15 hours. Poisoning can in fact be deadly if a mushroom that is consumed weighs about 50 g, which contains about 7 mg of amanitoxin.

The course of poisoning by Death Cap is as follows: the first signs appear 8 to 12 hours after the mushrooms have been eaten, although occasionally it may be even later, between 24 and 40 hours. Poisoning becomes evident through stomach aches, cold sweats, vomiting and diarrhoea. The abdomen becomes sensitive to pressure, the liver is swollen and urine is produced only in small quantities. Later the pains recede but periodically return. The patient is conscious throughout, but becomes weak; the heart-beat periodically falters, the limbs grow cold and the pulse is faint and irregular. The patient becomes unconscious in 2 to 3 days and dies in 5 to 10 days. The after-effects of even a slight poisoning last for a long time. Moreover, the poisonous attributes of the spores are not diminished by their age or lower temperatures. Experiments have proved that although high temperatures lessen the virulence of the poison, they do not destroy the toxic substances. Finally the dangerous character of the Death Cap arises from its long incubation period, during which the poison fully penetrates the blood stream so that any late stomach-pumping is ineffective.

Until recently, the medical profession was helpless in the face of such poisons. Neither the serum produced by vaccinating horses with extracts from the poisonous *Amanita* species nor injections of a glucose solution into the veins helped in any way; similarly valueless was the use of a mixture prepared from the minced raw stomachs and brains of rabbits. The important breakthrough came in 1959, when Dr. J. Herink from Prague advocated the administration of an octathionic (thiooktic) acid preparation, used as a cure for some liver diseases. Immediately three patients who had consumed Death Cap were saved. After 1959 this treatment, using preparations of octathionic acid, was further developed so that currently it is possible to cure all cases of poisoning by Death Cap, providing the nature of the poisoning is quickly established and the recognized procedures are employed. Dialysis on a kidney-machine has also recently been used with success.

The Destroying Angel *(Amanita virosa)* is another poisonous mushroom, although quite a rare species, which is distinguished from the other type of Death Cap *(A. phalloides* ssp. *verna)* by its sharp club-shaped cap and frayed stipe. It grows predominantly in mountain forests on a limestone subsoil. It is as potentially lethal as the Death Cap and its fruit-bodies contain another type of toxin called virosin, whose toxic effects can be compared with those of amanitoxins.

It should also be mentioned that amanitoxins are present in some other fungi, which are not necessarily related to the *Amanita* genus. These poisonous substances were for instance discovered in the fruit-bodies of a North American species called *Galerina marginata*. This is a small, rusty-brown Gill fungus which also grows in some European countries either singly or in clusters on rotten wood. It can quite easily be mistaken for the edible mushroom *Kuehneromyces mutabilis.*

The *Amanita* genus, however, contains some other definitely very poisonous species. These are the well-known Fly Agaric *(Amanita muscaria)*, which according to the most recent research contains many substances whose quantity and physiological effects are indeterminate and the poisoning from which shows itself in different ways. Long ago an extract from the fruit-body of this *Amanita* was mixed with sugar and used to kill flies. Fly Agaric has a stupefying effect and in some countries it is used as a narcotic. It resembles the deistic potion known as Soma, mentioned in the ancient Hindu Rig Veda, which dates back more than 3,000 years. It is also the same hallucinogenic drug which was used long ago in Siberia, Kamchatka and Chukotka by the indigenous population.

Fly Agaric contains muscarine in its fruit-bodies but only in small quantities and the poisonous consequences resulting from this are thus limited. However, the substance called cholin, which is a chemically related poison, is present in large quantities. The main poisonous substance present in the Fly Agaric is nevertheless iboten acid. Finally the general poisoning caused by the fruit-bodies of the European type of Fly Agaric can be recognized by general discomfort, an inclination to vomit, loss of vision and dizziness.

The Panther Cap *(Amanita pantherina)* occupies second place after the Death Cap in terms of the number of accidents caused by poisoning in the majority of European countries. In this instance the nature of the poisoning is similar to that caused by Fly Agaric, but it is stronger and more dangerous. The number of cases of poisoning caused by this *Amanita* has multiplied in recent years due to an increase in the collection of the Blusher mushroom *(A. rubescens)* and also occasionally that of *A. spissa.* A superficial knowledge of both species can easily deceive reckless mushroom-pickers and mistakes are made. Fortunately such poisoning seldom leads to death, although it reveals itself by affecting the nervous system, causing hallucinations, feverish excitement and irritation, and can eventually lead to loss of consciousness.

The *Inocybe* genus is also found to contain a number of poisonous toxins. However, poisoning by these fungi is a rare occurrence, because the majority of the species are very small and therefore do not readily attract the mushroom-picker's attention. An exception to this rule, however, is *Inocybe patouillardii*, which is quite a big and fleshy mushroom growing in calcareous soils under deciduous trees. The poisonous character of *Inocybe* is due to the presence of muscarine in their cell tissue, the alkaloid which was originally discovered in Fly Agaric. Muscarine poisoning is a strong irritant of the nervous system and is accompanied by perspiration, salivation and tears, diarrhoea, stomach aches, slowing down of the heart-beat, a drop in blood pressure and respiratory disorders. A fatal quantity of *I. patouillardii* can be reckoned as 500 g. This poisoning can be successfully cured by using atropine, which is the antidote for muscarine. This poisonous substance is also to be found in some *Clitocybe* species and in *Mycena pura*.

Poisoning of the digestive tract is commonplace and the symptoms are well known although the fungoid toxins which cause this are still an unknown quality. Some of them cause vomiting, others diarrhoea, some both. Again, some fungi are poisonous when they are raw, others when they are improperly cooked, others even when well cooked. Symptoms usually appear 2 to 4 hours after the food has been consumed. Of the fungi which cause such disorders in the digestive tract if consumed raw, perhaps *Clitocybe nebularis* is the best example and therefore it is not advisable to prepare salads of raw mushrooms. *Boletus satanas* is also very poisonous in its raw state. Just a small piece of this mushroom can cause violent vomiting which can last for several hours. Mild poisoning can be caused by the fruit-bodies of a number of other fungus species, such as *Boletus luridus*, *B. erythropus*, *B. variegatus*, by the acrid-tasting *Russula emetica* and *R. badia*, by the very bitter *Lactarius piperatus* and *L. torminosus*. Finally, an example of fungus which is poisonous when semi-raw is the Honey fungus *(Armillaria mellea)*.

Many species are poisonous even when well cooked, especially *Entoloma sinuosum* and *Tricholoma pardinum*. A milder poisoning can be caused by *Entoloma rhodopolium*, *E. nidorosum* and *E. ni-*

phoides, by *Tricholoma sejunctum* and *T. saponaceum*, which is often mistaken for *T. flavovirens*, and finally some brown varieties of Blewits *(T. flavobrunneum)*. Diarrhoea caused by *Nolanea verna* is relatively common in early spring. Again members of the *Scleroderma* genus (Earth-ball) when boiled in soup can cause vomiting and when cooked in fat, the after-effects are even stronger and require immediate medical treatment. Diarrhoea is also caused by *Ramaria formosa* (Fairy Clubs) and *R. mairei*, *Dermocybe sanguinea* and *D. malicoria*. The mild-tasting *Lactarius helvus* can also cause vomiting and the poisoning caused by some species of small *Lepiota (L. helveola*, *L. brunneoincarnata*, *L. scobinella* and others) is especially dangerous. Digestive disorders can even be caused by excellent edible mushrooms, such as *Boletus edulis*, if such mushrooms are collected in a plastic bag and subsequently sweat. Similarly, old, cooked mushrooms left in a warm place can cause indigestion if reheated; on the other hand, young and healthy mushrooms can be cooked, stored in a refrigerator and reheated again without adverse effect. Lastly, a number of tough mushrooms adversely effect the intestines, such as the Chantarelle *(Cantharellus cibarius)*.

Above all it is advisable not to drink alcohol after eating a number of mushroom species. The chemicals which they contain have a similar effect to preparations used in the treatment of alcoholism. They prevent the absorption of alcohol in the blood in the acetaldehyde phase, which usually causes a heavy heart-beat and a fear of death. Examples of such mushrooms are *Coprinus atramentarius* and *C. micaceus*.

By way of conclusion, mushrooms with hallucinogenic effects must also be noted. The majority of them originate in Mexico, where they were also botanically identified for the first time. However, chemicals having a narcotic effect were also discovered in some European genera, such as *Psilocybe* and *Panaeolus*.

HOW TO DEAL WITH MUSHROOM POISONING

In the first place a doctor should be called immediately. However, before his arrival, the patient should be made to vomit by touching the uvula, or by drinking lukewarm water with salt dissolved in it or another emetic. Stomach and abdominal pains can be soothed by a hot compress. If the patient is feverish, an icy compress should be placed on the forehead and the spine. Heart activity should be stimulated (if needed) by strong black coffee, or smelling salts. If the patient becomes unconscious, the face should be sprinkled with drops of cold water or he should be made to inhale ammonia fumes. Above all *alcoholic drinks must never be administered* by way of resuscitation! Finally it is essential to keep the vomited contents of the stomach for subsequent laboratory examination, in order to determine further medical treatment.

Symbols used: ☠ poisonous mushrooms

 ⊗ edible mushrooms

 ♟ inedible mushrooms

As an important means of identification, drawings of the spores are shown in the marginal notes, their real size being given in microns ($1\mu m = 1/1,000$ mm).

Peziza badioconfusa
Synonym: *Galactinia olivacea*

Peziza arvernensis

The fruit-bodies of the majority of Discomycetes are so small that they usually escape human attention. Exceptions are some genera of the order Pezizales, such as Morels *(Morchella)*, False Morels *(Helvella)*, *Gyromitra* and *Discina*. Also the *Peziza* genus includes some species with large. conspicuous fruit-bodies, to which the two illustrated here belong.

Peziza badioconfusa grows on bare, slightly damp ground close to woodland paths and streams. Its fruit-bodies are wide and cup-shaped and, when mature, if they are touched discharge clouds of whitish spore powder. This phenomenon is also characteristic of other related genera. A similar species, *Peziza badia*, is a deeper reddish-brown and the ornamentation of its spores is also different.

Peziza arvernensis is characterized by its spores, which have very fine warts. It usually grows under beech trees, hornbeams and oak trees, amongst their fallen leaves. *Peziza* species are inedible.

1 *P. badioconfusa:*
Fruit-body:
3–10 cm
in diameter.
Occurrence:
VI–IX.
Spores: 17.5–23×
8–10μm,
colourless.

2 *P. arvernensis:*
Fruit-body:
5–10 cm
in diameter.
Occurrence:
V–VIII.
Spores: 15–19×
7.5–11μm,
colourless.

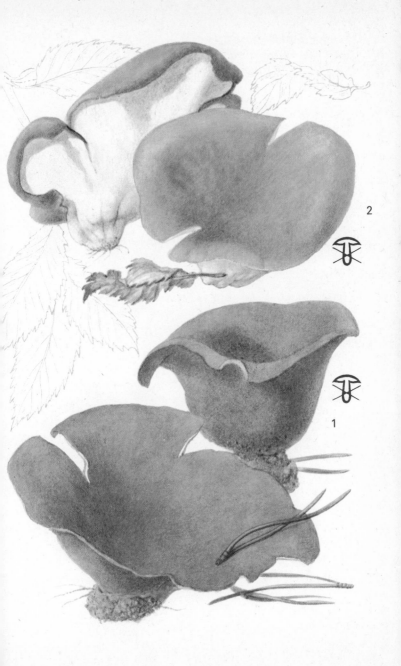

2

1

Helvella elastica
Synonym: *Leptopodia elastica*

Helvella acetabulum
Synonyms: *Acetabula vulgaris, Paxina acetabulum*

The fruit-body of False Morels is divided into a stipe, which is either rounded and smooth or longitudinally ribbed or furrowed, with a cup-shaped or saddle-shaped fertile head which is often irregularly lobed. The head of *Helvella elastica* is reminiscent of the shape of a riding saddle and in addition is divided into 2—3 lobes. It can be found growing in damp soil in various types of woodland.

Helvella acetabulum has deep, cup-shaped fruit-bodies which open gradually. Its prominent ribs, located on a relatively short stipe, branch out to the underside margins of its cup-shaped cap.

There also exist other species of this genus, the most frequently found being *Helvella crispa*, *H. lacunosa* and the minute *H. macropus*. Some of their common features are wide, ellipsoid and colourless spores which contain large drops of oil.

Some species with larger fruit-bodies are picked for food, such as *H. acetabulum*, but their flesh is thin and quite tough. They grow in masses among fallen leaves and needles.

1   *Helvella elastica*:
Cap: 2–4 cm in diameter.
Stipe: 3–10 cm high.
Occurrence: From summer to autumn.
Spores: 19–22× 11–13µm, colourless.

2   *Helvella acetabulum*:
Fruit-body: 4–8 cm in diameter.
Occurrence: V–VI.
Spores: 18–22× 12–14µm, colourless.

Staghorn fungus
Calocera viscosa

Pseudohydnum gelatinosum
Synonym: *Tremellodon gelatinosus*

The stumps of various tree species provide a habitat for this very extensive group of fungi. Many of them are minute, even microscopic, and so easily escape human attention, while others are striking in size, shape and colouring. One of the most abundant species is *Calocera viscosa*. Its shape is reminiscent of Fairy Clubs (Clavariaceae) and it can be easily mistaken for them, although they are not related. Its distinguishing features are its slimy, unusually springy and tough fruit-bodies, whose texture is neither fleshy nor crisp. *Calocera viscosa* is inedible; it grows on tree stumps, particularly those of spruce.

Pseudohydnum gelatinosum is characterized by its tough, gelatinous, tongue-shaped fruit-bodies and by the soft dense teeth on its underside. The colour of the fruit-bodies varies, ranging from pure milky-white and bluish shades to a dark amber-brown. *P. gelatinosum* is an edible species but due to its second-rate quality it is rarely collected. Usually it can be found growing on pine and spruce stumps.

1 *Calocera viscosa:*
Fruit-body:
2–7 cm high
Occurrence:
From summer to autumn.
Spores:
8–12×4–4,5μm, colourless.

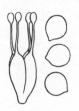

2 *Pseudohydnum gelatinosum:*
Fruit-body: 2–8 cm in diameter.
Occurrence:
From summer to autumn.
Spores:
5–7×4–6μm.

1

2

Jew's Ear

Hirneola auricula-judae

Tremella mesenterica
Exidia plana
Synonym: *Exidia glandulosa*

The three species illustrated here are the most abundant representatives of the two families of Basidiomycetes and the living fruit-bodies are strikingly resilient and gelatinous. The Jew's Ear likes to grow on the common elder and on false acacia. Its very supple fruit-bodies are bone hard when dry, but become pliable again when moistened. Some related species which grow in Asia are used in cooking. *Tremella mesenterica* is often found on the dead branches of deciduous trees, usually hornbeams and oaks. When moist its folded, brain-like, contorted fruit-bodies become bright yellow in colour. *Exidia plana* is even more common; it differs from other species of the *Exidia* genus by the presence of dark protrusions which are scattered over the surface of its blackish fruit-body. When dried out, it becomes narrow, black and shrivelled. Generally it grows on the cut surfaces of beech stumps and also on the branches and trunks of other trees lying on the ground. The Jew's Ear is edible, but *Tremella* and *Exidia* are not.

1 *Hirneola auricula-judae*: *Fruit-body*: 3–10 cm in diameter. *Occurrence*: Almost all the year round. *Spores*: 15–20×5–6µm, colourless.

2 *Tremella mesenterica*: *Fruit-body*: 2–4 cm in diameter. *Occurrence*: From spring to autumn. *Spores*: 10–12µm wide, colourless.

3 *Exidia plana*: *Fruit-body*: 3–10 cm in diameter. *Occurrence*: Mainly from autumn until spring. *Spores*: 10–16×4–5µm, colourless.

1

2

3

Inonotus hispidus

This Polypore is one of the most damaging but also prevalent members of this extensive family and lives on old trunks of fruit trees. Its fruit-bodies are juicy, meaty, heavy and very watery. The species is often characterized by large round pores in the form of tubular openings about 2—4 mm wide, which are interspersed with minute, rust-coloured pores, through which drops of a hot bitter liquid are excreted. The fruit-bodies also secrete surplus water in this way. These drops are best visible on young growths, which secrete large amounts of this liquid. This process takes place only in favourable damp weather conditons. The old dry fruit-bodies are hard, frail and almost black.

Inonotus hispidus is an annual fungus which attacks orchards with apple and occasionally pear trees, causing great damage. It prefers older trees as their central wooden column rots quickly. In the past a yellow dye has been produced from its fruit-bodies, used for painting and silk dying. In favourable conditions this fungus grows very fast, reaching a large size and weight, which can amount to as much as 5 kg when fresh. It is inedible.

Fruit-body:
8–35 cm
in diameter.
Occurrence:
Summer.
Spores:
7–12 × 6–9 μm,
yellow-brown.

Polyporus squamosus
Synonym: *Polyporellus squamosus*

This annual species is one of the largest of this family. Its semi-circular fruit-bodies are covered in brown apressed scales and its white, tough flesh, which is juicy when young, has a conspicuous cucumber-like, floury taste and scent. *Polyporus squamosus* is one of the few edible Polypores; mushroom-pickers consider its young fruit-bodies very tasty and pick them regularly. It is best used in soups. Old fruit-bodies are very tough and therefore not suitable for consumption. In size, shape and colouring *P. squamosus* varies considerably. It grows abundantly on the dead or living trunks or stumps of deciduous trees, especially of beech, willow, walnut, poplar, lime and ash. It also infests some decorative trees, such as the horse-chestnuts. Its fruit-bodies often grow in clusters at the base of tree trunks but also high above the ground on large branches. They grow very quickly after rain and reach a large size, weighing up to several kilograms. This is a harmful species in that it causes the white rot in wood. It is widespread in the temperate zones of the northern and southern hemispheres.

Cap: 5–60 cm in diameter.
Occurrence: From end of spring till August.
Spores: 10–14×4–5μm, colourless.

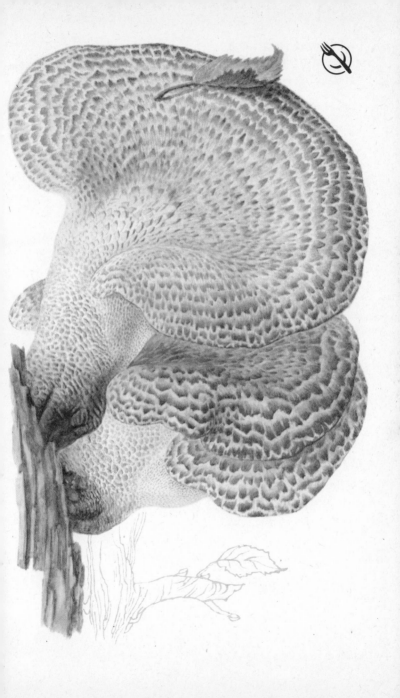

Boletus grevillei

Synonyms: *Suillus grevillei, Boletus elegans, Ixocomus elegans*

Boletus grevillei is an important member of the Boletaceae family, which is usually to be found under larch trees. It can be easily recognized by its orange or lemon-yellow cap which is slimy in damp weather. Its cuticle can be easily peeled off. The ring on its stipe is all that remains of the white or yellowish veil, which on young fruit-bodies entirely covers the lemon or chrome-yellow tubes. Its flesh has a pleasant, slightly resinous scent and when cut turns a light green. In favourable weather conditions this Boletus grows profusely under larch trees and is an excellent edible mushroom. The skin should be peeled off when the mushroom is picked because it is so slimy that everything in contact with it sticks to it. However, the skin of the young fruit-body is difficult to peel off and therefore the slime should at least be wiped off. *Boletus grevillei* is most suitable as an ingredient for soups and sauces, for pickling and also for frying with eggs. It is common in the temperate zones of the northern hemisphere, where it grows both in valleys as well as on mountain slopes throughout the whole larch distribution area.

There are other related species which also grow under larches, such as *Boletus granulatus, B. luteus, B. cavipes,* and the less common *Boletus aeruginascens.*

1   *Boletus grevillei:*
Cap: 4–12 cm in diameter.
Stipe: 5–10 cm high,
0.5–1.5 cm thick.
Occurrence:
From summer to autumn.
Spores:
10–12 × 3–4 μm, pale yellow.

Boletus scaber

Synonyms: *Leccinum scabrum,*
Krombholzia scabra

Mushroom-pickers often search for birch trees on
the edge of woods as they often find the fruit-bodies
of *Boletus scaber* and *Boletus versipellis* growing there.
Boletus scaber is the most common species of those
members of the Boletaceae family whose mycelia
grow in symbiosis with the roots of birch trees. Its
fruit-bodies can be found under old birches as well
as under young trees, in clearings as well as undergrowths in the temperate zones of the northern
hemisphere. Its cap, in various shades of grey to
brown, rests on a relatively thin and long white
stipe, covered with blackish scales. Its flesh is pure
white or off-white and does not change colour
when cut, although it turns black when dried out.
It has a pleasant and typical taste and scent.

Boletus scaber is a good edible mushroom, although its cap soon softens. However, its stipe is
too tough and woody to be consumed. Young
mushrooms are therefore best. Although its flesh
turns black during the cooking process, its flavour
is quite outstanding. It can be prepared in
a number of ways and its large fruit-bodies can
also be coated with breadcrumbs and fried.

Cap: 5–15 cm
in diameter.
Stipe:
6–15×1–1.5 cm.
Occurrence:
From summer
to autumn.
Spores:
13–18×5–6µm,
yellowish.

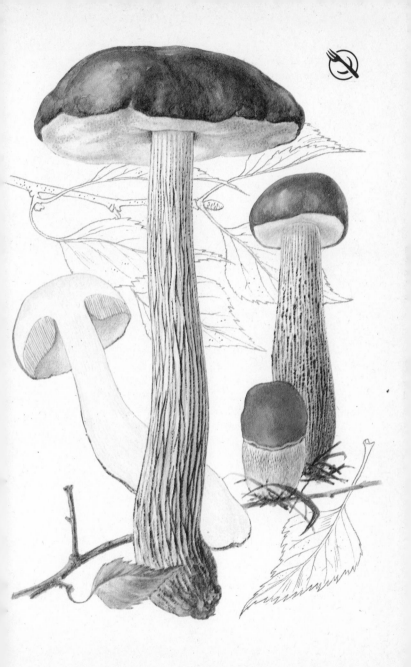

Boletus aurantiacus

Synonyms: *Leccinum aurantiacum,*
Krombholzia aurantiaca

Boletus aurantiacus, with its conspicuous red-orange cap, is a favourite mushroom because of its attractiveness and the decorative effect it creates in aspen and birch woods. It is dependent on aspen trees for its growth. Its most important features, which differentiate it from the similar *Boletus versipellis*, are the initially white, but later reddish-brown or brownish-orange scales on the stipe, its dark, brownish-red or reddish-brown cap and its whitish tubes. When cut, the flesh becomes greyish-pink and later turns black.

It is an excellent edible mushroom with an attractive appearance, and has the advantage of not being attacked by insect larvae. It can be prepared in a number of ways and is particularly suitable for coating in breadcrumbs. It is an important ingredient of some brown soups and can also be pickled in vinegar or salt. When used for cooking, the fruit-bodies are usually cut direct into the boiling water to stop their flesh turning black. It grows both in valleys and on mountain slopes in the temperate zones of the northern hemisphere.

Cap: 4–15 cm in diameter.
Stipe:
6–15 × 1–3 cm.
Occurrence:
From summer (sometimes as early as May) to autumn.
Spores:
13–16 × 4–5 μm, yellowish.

Boletus versipellis

Synonyms: *Leccinum versipelle,*
Krombholzia rufescens, Leccinum testaceoscabrum

Boletus versipellis is similar to the preceding species. It has a reddish-brown cap, but in contrast to *Boletus aurantiacus*, it grows predominantly under birch trees and also its cap is rather lighter in colour, and vividly brownish-orange or yellowish-brown; the scales on the stipe are black or brownish-black, the tubes are greyish even when young, and the originally whitish flesh becomes pink to greyish-violet when cut. The stipe at the base is a greenish-blue but this colouring is sometimes found in *Boletus aurantiacus* too.

This species is also a good edible mushroom, suitable for a number of cooking methods, and especially for frying in breadcrumbs. It is indigenous to the majority of countries in the temperate zone of the northern hemisphere, where it is always associated with birch trees.

There are, however, other species of this family which grow under other trees; for example *Leccinum vulpinum* is to be found under pine trees and *Leccinum piceum* under spruces. Their characteristic feature is a rusty, brownish-orange cap which is reminiscent in colour of *Lactarius rufus*.

Cap: 5–15 cm in diameter.
Stipe: 6–15 × 1–3 cm.
Occurrence: From summer to autumn.
Spores: 13–16 × 4–5 μm, yellow.

Boletus subtomentosus
Synonym: *Xerocomus subtomentosus*

Boletus chrysentereon
Synonym: *Xerocomus chrysentereon*

Both species can be found in large numbers in various types of woods even when other Boletus species are hard to find. However, because of their soft flesh (particularly *Boletus chrysentereon*), they do not transport very well and are often attacked by other fungi which cover them with mould.

Boletus subtomentosus, which is tougher than *B. chrysentereon*, is more popular with mushroom-pickers, though one species is often mistaken for the other. The cap of *Boletus subtomentosus* does not crack and the layer of flesh immediately under its cuticle does not contain the carmine-red pigment; its pores are a deep chrome-yellow and the stipe is usually ribbed at the top and tapers downwards. *Boletus chrysentereon*, which may vary greatly in appearance, can usually be identified only by the surface cracks in the cuticle of the cap, which reveals a carmine-red pigment. The presence of this pigment can also be detected in fruit-bodies which have not cracked, simply by carefully scratching the skin surface. The tubes of this Boletus are pale yellow, sometimes greenish-yellow, whilst the stipe is cylindrical and tapering towards the base, usually without ribs and reddish in some places.

1   *Boletus subtomentosus:*
Cap: 4–10 cm in diameter.
Stipe: 3–8 × 1–2 cm.
Occurrence: From summer to autumn.
Spores: 12–14 × 5–6 μm, pale yellow.

2   *Boletus chrysentereon:*
Cap: 3–8 cm in diameter.
Stipe: 3–6 × 0.7–1.8 cm.
Occurrence: From summer to autumn.
Spores: 13–15 × 4–6 μm, pale yellow.

1

2

Boletus badius

Synonyms: *Xerocomus badius, Ixocomus badius*

Boletus badius can be easily recognized by its chestnut or chocolate-brown, smooth cap, which is slightly sticky in damp conditions. Its pores are pale, later becoming yellowish to yellowish-green, and turn green when bruised. The flesh is whitish, although it turns blue when cut. The pale brown stipe is cylindrical, often curved and tapering at the base. It has a pleasant mushroom scent and taste.

Cap: 5–12 cm in diameter.
Stipe: 3–8 × 1.5–3 cm.
Occurrence: From summer to late autumn.
Spores: 12–16 × 4–6 μm, pale yellow-brown.

Boletus badius is widespread in coniferous forests, particularly in mountainous regions. Sometimes it grows directly from the base of tree trunks or rotting stumps or even from rotten spruce cones, which have been penetrated through the soil by the mycelium. It can often be found on the margins of woods, concealed in short grass. In some regions it grows in clumps in spruce and pine forests. It is a popular edible mushroom, its main advantages being that it can still be found up until late autumn and that it is only rarely attacked by insect larvae. It cannot be mistaken for any other species, perhaps except for *Tylopilus felleus*, which also grows prolifically in coniferous forests, but which has a lighter cap with a conspicuous network of veins on its stipe and pinkish tubes. Its flesh does not turn blue when cut and it has a repulsive bitter taste. *Boletus badius* is good for soups, sauces, and for frying and pickling in vinegar and salt.

Boletus cavipes

Synonym: *Boletinus cavipes*

Boletus variegatus
Synonym: *Suillus variegatus, Ixocomus variegatus*

Boletus cavipes can be easily recognized by the shape of its fruit-bodies, as well as by its habitat, because it is invariably associated with larch trees and sometimes even grows under isolated trees which often line woodland paths. On the whole it prefers mountainous regions with a clay soil. The colouring of its cap varies; sometimes it is a pale lemon or an orange yellow; at other times it is a vivid reddish-brown. Its characteristic features are a felt-like, scaled cap which is soft and flexible, a hollow stipe and large, elongated pores arranged in rays. These converge on the stipe and are covered by a white veil when young. In taste and scent it is somewhat inconspicuous.

However, it is a relatively good edible mush-room, suitable for soups and for frying with scrambled eggs. As dishes prepared of *Boletus cavipes* have a slightly astringent taste, it is better mixed with other mushrooms (e.g. with *Boletus grevillei*).

Boletus variegatus grows in pine forests on acid, non-calcareous and especially sandy soils. It often grows in large numbers and in some regions is quite popular. Its young fruit-bodies are particularly substantial and tasty. It is a useful ingredient for soups, sauces and is also good pickled in vinegar.

1 *Boletus cavipes:*
Cap: 3–12 cm in diameter.
Stipe: 3–6 × 0.5–1.5 cm.
Occurrence: VII–X.
Spores: 8–10 × 3–4 μm, pale yellow.

2 *Boletus variegatus:*
Cap: 5–12 cm in diameter.
Stipe: 5–10 × 1–3 cm.
Occurrence: VIII–X.
Spores: 8–10 × 3.5–4 μm, pale green-yellow.

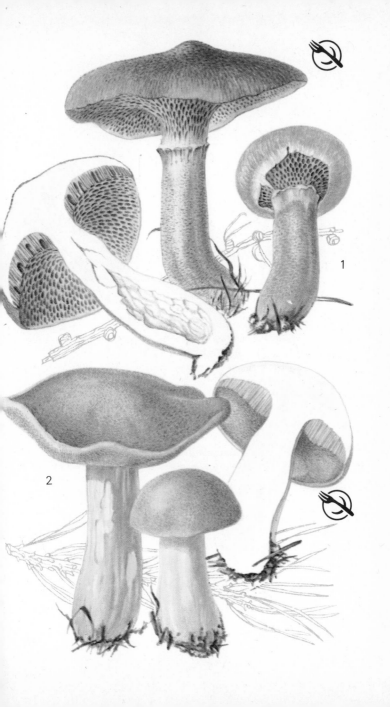

1
2

Boletus satanas

Boletus calopus
Synonym: *Boletus pachypus*

The true *Boletus satanas* is a sturdy mushroom with a light grey or silvery-brown cap. Its yellow tubes have deep carmine-red pores and the central section of its carmine stipe is decorated with a fine network of veins. Its flesh becomes pale blue when cut but this colouring later disappears. It also has an unpleasant sweaty smell, but its taste is pleasant and reminiscent of hazelnuts. *Boletus satanas* is a relatively rare mushroom growing exclusively in a calcareous soil in deciduous woods, mostly with oaks and hornbeams or limes and hazel bushes. It is extremely poisonous when raw — a small piece of it can cause persistent vomiting.

Boletus calopus has pale yellow tubes, whilst its stipe is yellow at the apex, red in the centre and covered by a veined network at the base. Its very bitter flesh turns blue when cut, but later loses colour and becomes a dirty greyish-yellow. As a result of its bitter taste, *Boletus calopus* is not regarded as edible. It grows in coniferous and occasionally deciduous forests and is particularly prevalent in mountainous regions. *Boletus calopus* can be mistaken for the edible *Boletus luridus*, which is not bitter and whose tubular pores are red.

1 *Boletus satanas:*
Cap: 10–20 cm in diameter.
Stipe: 5–12 × 3–6 cm.
Occurrence: VII–VIII.
Spores: 10–15 × 6–7 μm, pale yellowish.

2 *Boletus calopus:*
Cap: 6–12 cm in diameter.
Stipe: 3–8 × 2–5 cm.
Occurrence: From summer to autumn.
Spores: 10–13 × 4–5 μm, pale yellowish.

Boletus edulis
Synonyms: *Boletus bulbosus*
Boletus edulis ssp. *bulbosus*

Boletus aestivalis
Synonyms: *Boletus edulis* ssp. *reticulatus*
Boletus reticulatus

Both of the species illustrated are the most common and usually the most popular edible mushrooms. The difference between the species are only marginal. *Boletus edulis* has a light to dark chestnut-brown, smooth cap, whilst its tubes are white at first and yellow-green later. The stipe is also white but later changes to a tan colour; it has a less noticeable network of veins than *Boletus aestivalis*. The flesh is a constant white and has a sweet taste and a pleasant mushroom aroma. The colour of the cap of *Boletus aestivalis* ranges from a greyish-ochre, pale brown or light greyish-brown to a leather-brown along its entire length and has a conspicuous large, square-patterned network. Its other features are similar to those of *Boletus edulis*.

While *Boletus edulis* grows mainly in coniferous forests, especially in undergrowths of young spruce or along the forest boundary and on forest paths in a rather acid soil, *Boletus aestivalis* usually appears in oak and beech woods or even under single oak trees growing near ponds. Occasionally it is found growing under other deciduous trees (e.g. under beeches) in low-lying and warm regions. It is very rarely found in coniferous forests.

Both species are among the most sought after and delicious mushrooms, which can be prepared in the kitchen in a number of ways.

1 *Boletus edulis:*
Cap: 5–20 cm
in diameter.
Stipe:
5–15×2.5–4 cm.
Occurrence:
VII—X.
Spores:
15–17×4–5μm,
olive-brown.

2 *Boletus aestivalis:*
Cap: 5–18 cm
in diameter.
Stipe:
5–15×3–5 cm.
Occurrence:
V–VIII.
Spores:
14–16×4–5μm,
olive-brownish.

2

Synonym: *Boletus felleus*

Tylopilus felleus might be called a twin of *Boletus edulis*. They often grow together in spruce forests and therefore they can be easily mistaken for one another. Both mushrooms are similar in the shape and colouring of their fruit-bodies and so it is not surprising if a mushroom-picker gathers *Tylopilus felleus* only to realize his mistake when eating a dish prepared from it. For *Tylopilus felleus* has a very strong, repulsively acrid taste and can be recognized immediately in any mixture of mushrooms. However, this mistake can be avoided if some care is taken. *Tylopilus felleus* is characterized not only by its bitter taste, but also by its pale pink tubes which, when bruised or old, become a rusty brown and are never yellow-green like the tubes of the ripe fruit-bodies of *Boletus edulis*. These tubes are at first white and angular, whilst the stipe is covered by a network of veins. The pinkish colouring of the tubes is related to the pink colour of the spore powder. It is as a result of this feature that the *Tylopilus* genus was established and *Tylopilus felleus* is one of its members. The species is slightly poisonous. It often grows in large numbers in damp coniferous forests and on the slopes of mountains. It may also be found around the rotten stumps of spruce trees. Finally it prefers an acid, non-calcareous soil.

Cap: 5–12 cm in diameter.
Stipe: 4–12 > 1–5 cm.
Occurrence: VI–X.
Spores: 12–18 × 3–4.5 μm, pale pinkish, almost colourless.

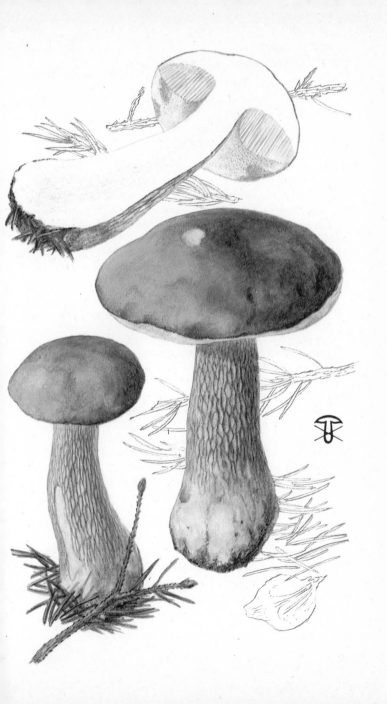

Ramaria aurea
Synonym: *Clavaria aurea*

Clavariadelphus ligula
Synonym: *Clavaria ligula*

The shape of the fruit-bodies of Fairy Clubs (Clavariaceae) is similar to that of sea corals. They are usually multi-branched at the base and sometimes form large clusters in which various shades of yellow predominate. *Ramaria aurea* provides an attractive decoration for deciduous woods. Their golden yellow or chrome-yellow and later ochre-yellow branches differ from those of the similar species, *Ramaria flava*, which has a sulphur-yellow colour, and *Ramaria formosa*, which is a pale salmon-pink with only the tips of its branches being ochre-yellow. These species can also be found both in deciduous woods and in coniferous forests. *Ramaria aurea* is edible, but because it is difficult to distinguish from other similar species which are slightly poisonous (e.g. *Ramaria formosa*, whose flesh is slightly bitter), it is best avoided in cooking. The surface of the branches of ripe fruit-bodies is covered with a yellow powder of spores.

Some Fairy Clubs have the shape of a simple club. One such species, which is particularly prolific, is *Clavariadelphus ligula*. Sometimes it grows in large quantities amongst rotting needles in spruce forests. It is inedible and tastes bitter.

1 Ramaria aurea:
Fruit-body: Up to 15 cm high.
Occurrence:
From summer to autumn.
Spores:
8–15×3–6μm, pale yellow.

2 Clavariadelphus ligula:
Fruit-body:
3–8 cm high, 5–8 mm thick.
Occurrence:
VIII–X.
Spores:
10–15×5–6μm, colourless.

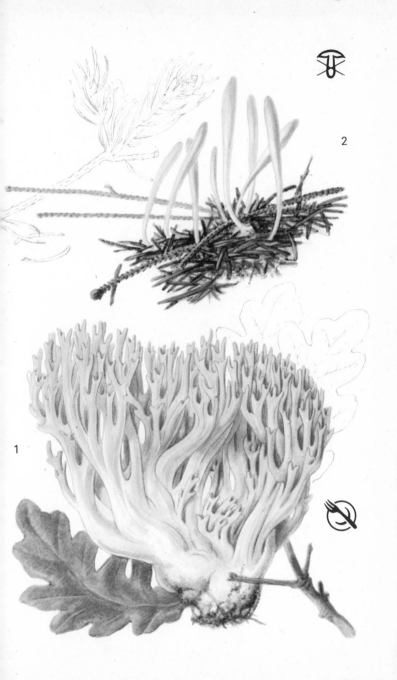

Gomphidius glutinosus
Synonym: *Leucogomphidius glutinosus*

The fruit-bodies of this fungus, covered with a thick layer of gelatinous slime, appear after rain at the end of the summer and in the autumn. At first sight they are reminiscent of *Boletus grevillei*, with which they share many common characteristics and a similar habitat. They are closely related to the Boletaceae family. The distinguishing feature is gills instead of tubes on the underside of the cap which are quite shallow and flexible and joined to the stipe. They are at first whitish, but later grey or black. The young fruit-bodies are covered with a transparent gelatinous veil, which remains visible on the adult fruit-bodies in the form of a risen ring on the stipe immediately below the gills. When dry the fruit-bodies are shiny.

Gomphidius glutinosus is quite common and it lives in mycorrhiza with woodland trees, especially conifers. It is edible and very tasty, especially when pickled in vinegar. It is native to the whole of the temperate zone of the northern hemisphere in coniferous forests.

Cap: 5–12 cm in diameter.
Stipe: 4–10 × 1–1.5 cm.
Occurrence: VIII–X.
Spores: 16–22 × 5–7.5 μm, brown.

Gomphidius rutilus
Synonym: *Gomphidius viscidus*

Gomphidius rutilus, the second most populous member of this family, is generally to be found in pine forests. Unlike *Gomphidius glutinosus*, this species is only slightly slimy or sticky when it is damp. It is characterized by its yellow-brown to orange-yellow cap with a point or 'umbo' in the centre and by the yellowish to yellow-orange gills, which turn black with spore powder during the adult stage and are joined to the stipe. The stipe is similar in colour to the cap and has a very faint ring near the top. An interesting microchemical reaction can be observed on the flesh of fresh fruit-bodies: if a drop of soda solution comes into contact with its flesh, which is originally orange-yellow, it turns violet; if coated with a solution of green vitriol it becomes deep green and in contact with a weak solution of ammonia it turns a vivid carmine. A change in the colour of the flesh is also noticeable when the fruit-body is drying out, during which process both the skin on the cap and stipe as well as the flesh itself turn pink.

Like *Gomphidius glutinosus*, *Gomphidius rutilus* is also an excellent edible mushroom and can be prepared in a number of ways. It turns violet when boiled and when pickled in vinegar it becomes almost black. This is a useful feature as it adds to the varied colour of any mushroom mixture.

Cap: 5–13 cm in diameter.
Stipe: 5–10 × 0.5–1 cm.
Occurrence: From summer to autumn.
Spores: 18–24 × 6–7 μm, dark blackish-brownish.

Paxillus involutus
Paxillus atrotomentosus

Paxillus involutus is one of the most abundant mushrooms. Its cap is viscid in the centre and woolly at the edges and in colour is almost identical to its short stipe. The yellowish flesh has a slightly bitter taste and smell. If it is bruised the whole fruit-body turns a rust colour and later brown. *Paxillus involutus* grows in a variety of woods, is especially prolific under birch trees, but also under isolated trees in lanes and parkland from valleys right up to high mountain slopes. This mushroom used to be considered edible, was regularly cropped and used in cooking. However, it has now been shown that *Paxillus involutus* is in fact poisonous. Particularly when eaten repeatedly it leads to the formation of antidotes in the human body. These have an adverse effect on the body in the long run and can cause allergies and the wastage of red blood cells. It is recommended therefore that *Paxillus involutus* should not be collected.

Paxillus atrotomentosus is often seen on the stumps and dead roots of coniferous trees. It is not poisonous, but is a poor quality. The taste and smell of its flesh is bitter and acidic.

1   Paxillus involutus:
Cap: 5–15 cm.
Stipe:
3–10×1–2 cm.
Occurrence:
From June till
late autumn.
Spores:
8–10×4–6μm,
yellow-brown.

2   Paxillus atrotomentosus:
Cap: 6–20 cm
in diameter.
Stipe:
2–6×2–3 cm.
Occurrence:
From summer
to autumn.
Spores:
5–6×3–4μm,
yellow-brown.

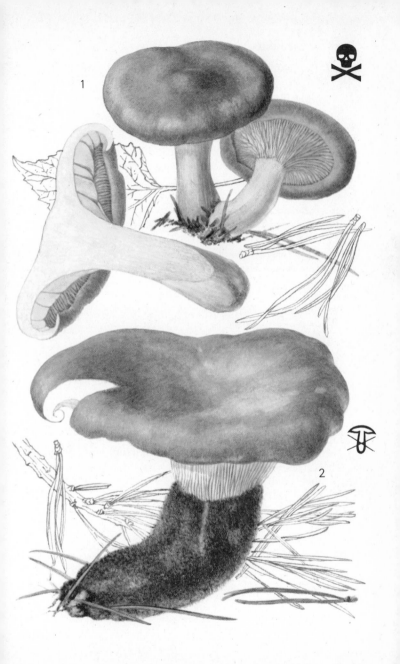

Honey fungus

Armillaria mellea
Synonym: *Armillariella mellea*

Pholiota squarrosa

There are not many other mushrooms as common as the Honey fungus. In September its clusters usually cover the stumps, roots and bases of live or dying deciduous or coniferous trees. Less frequently it occurs as early as June. It is a dangerous parasite which damages fruit trees as well as many woodland species. When tree trunks are attacked, they become covered with white sheets of mycelia or with multi-branched ribbons of this fungus, which are brown or black on the surface and white inside and which penetrate the bark and base of the tree.

The Honey fungus is a popular, edible species in some regions and is found in large quantities. Its young fruit-bodies are collected whole, but in older specimens only the caps can be used. It is one of the best mushrooms for pickling in vinegar and can also be added to soups and sauces or fried. However, raw or inadequately cooked fruit-bodies can cause indigestion.

Inexperienced mushroom-pickers sometimes confuse the Honey fungus with *Pholiota squarrosa*, which grows in similar habitats. Fortunately it is not poisonous, but tough and indigestible. This mushroom can be easily recognized by its sharp scales, the scaly ring on its stipe and its rusty brown spore powder.

1   Armillaria mellea:
Cap: 5–15 cm in diameter.
Stipe: 5–20×1–2.5 cm.
Occurrence: Mostly autumn, particularly September.
Spores: 6–8×3.5–4μm, colourless.

1   Pholiota squarrosa:
Cap: 3–12 cm in diameter.
Stipe: 6–15×1–2 cm.
Occurrence: From summer to autumn.
Spores: 7–9×5–6μm, ochre-brown.

1

2

Parasol mushroom

Lepiota procera

Agaricaceae

Shaggy Parasol

Lepiota rhacodes.

The large and elegant fruit-bodies of the Parasol mushroom often grow gregariously at the height of the summer season in the dry areas of spruce forests and other woodlands, especially near their sunlit edges and in clearings. This conspicuous mushroom, which is one of the largest gill fungi, has a veiled cap when young, shaped like a club, but later opening out like a parasol. Its surface is covered with large, dark scales, the surface of the stipe has brown transverse stripes and a loose, double collar-like ring.

The Shaggy Parasol, which grows in summer and autumn in dry woods, copses, parks and gardens, can easily be distinguished from the Parasol mushroom by its smooth, stripe-free stipe and the colour changes of its flesh. If the surface of the stipe is scratched, especially near the base, it soon turns a saffron-yellow, which later becomes a reddish-brown. This change of colour can best be observed on fresh fruit-bodies. Finally the cap of the Shaggy Parasol is not as scaly as that of the true Parasol mushroom. It sometimes grows on the nests of wood ants.

Both species are edible but to ensure the best quality, only young specimens should be picked when their caps are still enclosed or only half open. Both these fungi are excellent for all culinary purposes and have a very fine flavour.

1   *Lepiota procera:*
Cap: 10–25 cm in diameter.
Stipe:
15–40 × 2–4 cm.
Occurrence:
From late summer to autumn.
Spores:
16–20 × 10–13 μm, colourless.

2   *Lepiota rhacodes:*
Cap: 10–15 cm in diameter.
Stipe:
5–10 × 1–2.5 cm.
Occurrence:
From summer to autumn.
Spores:
9–12 × 6–7 μm, colourless.

1

2

Russula foetens
Russula ochroleuca

Numerically speaking the genus *Russula* is one of the largest among the gill fungi. There are at least 100 species found in Europe. The two illustrated species are more or less yellow in colour, bitter in taste and therefore inedible. The *Russula* genus along with the *Lactarius* genus are the only kind of fungi whose poisonous nature can be detected simply by taste. For cooking purposes only the mild species are gathered, whose flesh does not cause a burning sensation on the tongue.

Russula foetens is a common species distributed in all types of woods, but largely found in spruce forests on an acid soil. The young fruit-bodies with their enclosed, globular cap, pressed firmly to the stipe, are reminiscent of the young *Boletus edulis*, but its gills and tan-coloured stipe soon reveal this mushroom's identity. Old fruit-bodies have the strong unpleasant smell of burnt oil and therefore cannot be mistaken for other mushrooms.

Russula ochroleuca has a smooth, yellow or yellow-ochre, groove-free cap. It grows gregariously in mountainous spruce forests towards the end of summer and in autumn. It has almost no smell, but because of its acrid taste is not collected.

1 Russula foetens:
Cap: 6–16 cm in diameter.
Stipe:
2–6 × 1.5–3 cm.
Occurrence:
From summer to autumn.
Spores:
8–10 × 8–9 μm, yellowish.
Spore powder pale yellowish.

2 Russula ochroleuca:
Cap: 5–18 cm in diameter.
Stipe:
4–15 × 3–4 cm.
Occurrence:
From August to October.
Spores:
8–11 × 8–10 μm, yellowish.
Spore powder pale yellowish.

1

2

Some *Russula* species are unusually variable. One of these is *Russula cyanoxantha*, which grows in deciduous and coniferous forests. Its cap is relatively large and has a supple fleshy texture which is a cloudy violet or purple-blue. However, other specimens are frequently green in colour; the centre of the cap can in fact be almost dark green, whilst at other times the whole cap is pink to lilac in places. Although the colour of this species can vary a great deal, it can be easily identified by one feature, which is particularly characteristic of *Russula cyanoxantha*: its gills seem greasy when touched, are also pliable and therefore do not fracture as often happens in other species of this genus. Its stipe is normally pure white and remains so, as do its gills. If the cap of a fresh specimen is cut away from the stipe and placed on a sheet of black paper with its gills facing down, the paper will be covered in a few hours with spores in the form of a chalky white powder. The colour of this spore dust is an important attribute in identifying individual *Russula* species. Another important feature is the very finely wrinkled cuticle of the cap and the pleasant taste of the odourless flesh. It is in fact a good edible species.

Cap : 5–15 cm in diameter.
Stipe : 3–10 × 1.5–2.5 cm.
Occurrence : From June to October.
Spores : 7–10 × 7–8 μm, colourless. Spore powder pure white.

Russula emetica
Russula lepida

The vivid red colouring of some *Russula* species gives a lively decorative effect to coniferous forests at the height of summer and the beginning of autumn. One of the most abundant of them is *Russula emetica*, which is very bitter, inedible and formerly considered poisonous. It can be identified by its pure white spore powder, which also whitens the gills for a long time. The flesh is delicate and has a strong, sour, fruity smell. It is inadvisable to eat it, although experiments done by some mycologists have shown that it is harmless when cooked. However, it may cause a violent attack of vomiting if swallowed raw.

Unlike *Russula emetica*, *Russula lepida* is a mushroom that likes a dry atmosphere. It grows particularly in dry, pine forests but also in mixed woodlands. It prefers a light sunny position and its fruit-bodies occur in dry weather when other mushrooms are not to be seen. This *Russula* has a hard and firm flesh with a distinctive mild and resinous taste, reminiscent of menthol. Its impressive pink-vermilion cap has a dull-coloured cuticle, which in places has a white 'bloom'. Part of the stipe's surface is the same colour as the cap, from whose cuticle a red pigment passes along to the gill edges. It should not be eaten.

1   Russula emetica:
Cap: 4–8 cm in diameter.
Stipe: 4–10×1–2 cm.
Occurrence: From summer to autumn (VII–X).
Spores: 8–11×8–9μm. Spore powder white.

2   Russula lepida:
Cap: 4–10 cm in diameter.
Stipe: 4–8×1.5–2.5 cm.
Occurrence: VII–IX.
Spores: 8–9×7–8μm. Spore powder pale yellowish.

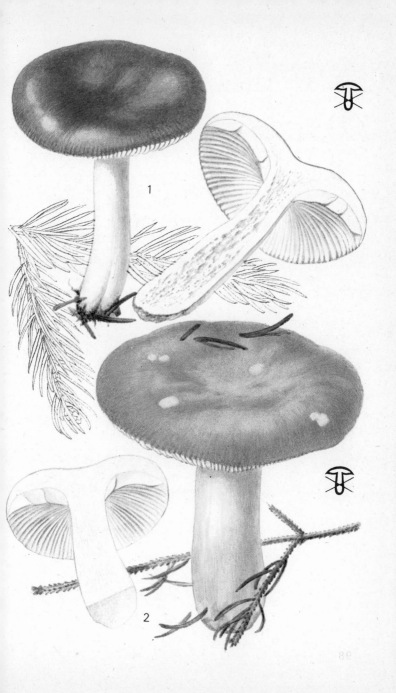

Russula vesca
Russula paludosa

In culinary terms *Russula vesca*, which grows in dry, mixed woodlands, is the tastiest of all the *Russula* species. The sweet taste of its flesh is similar to that of almonds or hazelnuts. Rust-coloured patches appear on its fruit-bodies if they are bruised. A close relative of *Russula vesca* is *Russula heterophylla*, the cap of which is coloured in various shades of green or yellow-green. The flesh of both species turns orange or almost red when it comes into contact with a solution of green vitriol. *Russula paludosa*, from the standpoint of taste, also belongs to the best *Russula* species. Its correct identification requires some experience, as it can be easily mistaken for some other red *Russula* species which have an acrid taste. It grows comparatively tall and its nicely coloured cap reminds one of ripe rosehips or strawberries. The cap, however, often loses colour and turns from an orange to a creamy yellow. This mushroom gives some colour to damp pine and mossy spruce forests, largely in mountainous areas, where it can often be found growing in large clusters. It also likes to grow near bilberry bushes and in peat bogs. Its flesh has a pleasant, mild taste.

1 Russula vesca:
Cap: 5–8 cm
in diameter.
Stipe:
3–7 × 1.5–2.5 cm.
Occurrence:
From summer
to autumn.
Spores:
6–8 × 5–6 μm,
colourless.
Spore powder
white.

2 Russula
paludosa:
Cap: 6–15 cm
in diameter.
Stipe:
7–18 × 1.5–2.5 cm.
Occurrence:
From June
to September.
Spores:
9–12 × 8–9 μm,
pale yellow.
Spore powder
pale ochre.

The green colouring of gill fungi should always provide a clear warning for mushroom-pickers who are basically unfamiliar with individual species, are inexpert in their identification yet still want to pick mushrooms for cooking purposes, as the most poisonous mushroom, the Death Cap *(Amanita phalloides)*, has a green cap. Many mistakes, with tragic consequences, have originated from an inability to distinguish *Russula virescens* or some other similarly coloured species (e.g. *Russula aeruginea)* from the Death Cap. A distinguishing characteristic is that the edible *Russula*, unlike the Death Cap, has no volva at the base of the stipe, nor a ring on the stipe below the cap. However, an experienced mushroom-picker, who can rely on his expertise and distinguish the *Russula* species from *Amanita*, can enrich his mushroom collection with this species. *Russula virescens* can be recognized by its verdigris green or greyish-green cap, which loses colour and grows pale, and by its cuticle that breaks soon into areolate patches. This mushroom is a relatively sturdy species with firm flesh and a wide-rounded cap. Its gills, stipe and flesh are white but inclined to turn a tan colour. A drop of green vitriol turns the flesh of its fresh fruit-bodies a deep red. This edible and delicious tasting *Russula* species is fond of dry, light, deciduous and coniferous woods, where it likes to grow alongside grassy paths.

Cap: 5–12 cm in diameter.
Stipe: 3–9×2–5 cm.
Occurrence: From summer to autumn.
Spores: 8–10×7–8μm, colourless. Spore powder white or whitish.

Often in spring, clusters of apparently old, black
and mummified fruit-bodies can be seen in some
woods and a careful examination will relate them
to the *Russula* genus. Usually they are the car-
pophores of *Russula nigricans*. The sturdy fruit-
bodies of this mushroom can survive for a long
time in woods and are not as susceptible to decay
as other fleshy mushrooms. It has strikingly sparse,
thick fragile gills. The flesh of its fresh fruit-body
turns a brick red when cut or bruised, and later
turns grey and black. The flesh of its relative,
Russula adusta, which grows regularly in pine
forests, does not turn red, but becomes immediately brown and black. The gills of both species
also differ; in *Russula adusta* they are much closer
together than in *Russula nigricans*.

Both these species of *Russula* are edible and in
some regions are very popular. However, their
quality is not really good and their flesh is tough
and has an unpleasant, earthy smell.

Cap: 8–20 cm
in diameter.
Stipe:
4–10×2–3.5 cm.
Occurrence:
From summer
to autumn.
Spores:
6–8×6–7 μm.
Spore powder
pure white.

The colour of *Russula xerampelina* should be reminiscent of the autumn shades of vine leaves and grapes, but in fact is very chameleon-like in character. Many specimens range in colour from shades of red, blue and violet, to brown and green and even yellow and orange. Several colours can sometimes be present in a single specimen. All these colour deviations, however, are balanced by certain common features, by which *Russula xerampelina* can be safely identified. These include the fact that the stipe and later the whole fruit-body becomes yellowish-brown to brown when bruised, whilst when it is old and starting to fade away, its fruit-bodies smell of pickled herring (trimethylamin). Finally a solution of green vitriol turns the flesh green as opposed to the majority of other *Russula* species, where the change is to a pink or grey colour. *Russula xerampelina* is sometimes compared with *Lactarius volemus* because of its similarity in smell. It is edible and grows in all types of woods.

Russula badia, found growing in coniferous forests, is one of the most acrid mushrooms. Even a small piece in the mouth can cause a long-lasting, burning sensation. Another characteristic feature is the cedar-like scent, which is similar to that of wooden pencils or fresh peaty moss. The deep reddish-brown or cloudy violet to violet-brown cap is almost black in the centre, the stipe has a pinkish hue and the flesh turns a rusty colour when bruised.

1   *Russula
xerampelina:*
Cap: 4–12 cm
in diameter.
Stipe:
4–6 × 1.5–3 cm.
Occurrence:
VII–X.
Spores:
8–13 × 8–12 μm.
Spore powder
pale ochre.

2   *Russula badia:*
Cap: 6–12 cm
in diameter.
Stipe:
5–10 × 1.5–2.5 cm.
Occurrence:
VIII–X.
Spores:
8–11 × 7–8 μm.
Spore powder
yellow.

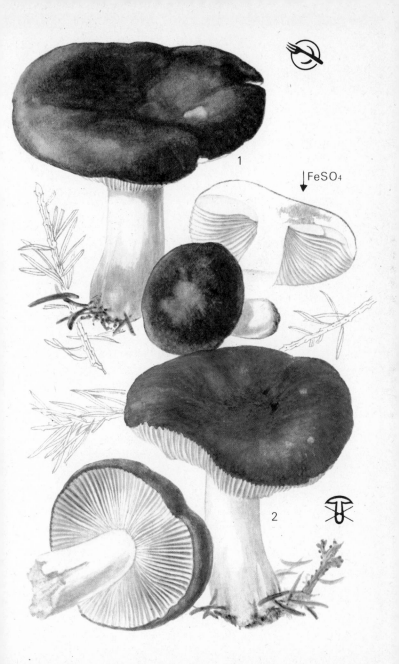

1

↓FeSO₄

2

Lactarius helvus

Lactarius rufus

A common feature of all *Lactarius* species is the presence of a milky latex in the flesh of its fruit-bodies, which trickles away when the mushroom is cut or broken. Its milky colour and the colour changes that take place when it is exposed to the air, as well as its taste, are the most important distinguishing features of the individual *Lactarius* species. Some species can also be safely identified by their distinctive smell. *Lactarius helvus* grows in damp coniferous woods. It is poisonous and if consumed, causes vomiting, acute diarrhoea and perspiration.

Lactarius rufus is one of the commonest mushrooms of the conifer forests. It appears in large numbers and grows in circles amongst the rotting needles of spruce trees. It grows even in summer when other mushrooms are normally scarce. As a result it is to be found in dry forests. It is not poisonous, but is not gathered because of its bitter taste and second-rate quality. Inexperienced mushroom pickers may confuse it with *Lactarius volemus*.

1   *Lactarius helvus:*
Cap: 5–12 cm in diameter.
Stipe: 4–10×1–1.5 cm.
Occurrence: VII–X.
Spores: 6.5–9× 5.5–6.5 μm, colourless.

2   *Lactarius rufus:*
Cap: 3–8 cm in diameter.
Stipe: 3–8×0.5–1 cm.
Occurrence: V–X.
Spores: 8–9.5× 6.5–7.5 μm, colourless.

1

2

Lactarius deliciosus
Cantharellus cibarius

Lactarius deliciosus is one of the well known, traditionally picked edible mushrooms. It is best when pickled in vinegar, but it can also be suitably prepared in other ways. It has a pleasant spicy flavour and scent. Its advantage is that it can be easily recognized and cannot be mistaken for any poisonous species. A typical specimen has an orange-red or ochre-orange cap with greenish stains; when cut it produces a carrot-orange milk, which turns green when it dries out. Its gills also turn green when bruised. *Lactarius deliciosus* grows predominantly in grass and moss under young spruce trees, in woodland glades and at the edges of woods.

Cantharellus cibarius is one of the most abundant and most often collected mushrooms. It grows from May to November on moss or among fallen leaves in both deciduous and coniferous woods. It occurs throughout the whole temperate zone of the northern hemisphere as well as in north Africa and Australia.

Cantharellus cibarius can be easily identified by its typical yellow fruit-bodies. The underside of the cap is covered with gill-like fertile folds. It has a pleasant spicy taste and is well suitable for a number of cooking methods.

1 *Lactarius deliciosus:*
Cap: 3–10 cm in diameter.
Stipe: 2–5 × 1–2 cm.
Occurrence: From end of summer to autumn.
Spores: 7–9 × 6–7 μm, colourless.

2 *Cantharellus cibarius:*
Cap: 1–8 cm in diameter.
Stipe: 2–4 × 0.5–2 cm.
Occurrence: From summer to autumn.
Spores: 7–9 × 4–5 μm, colourless.

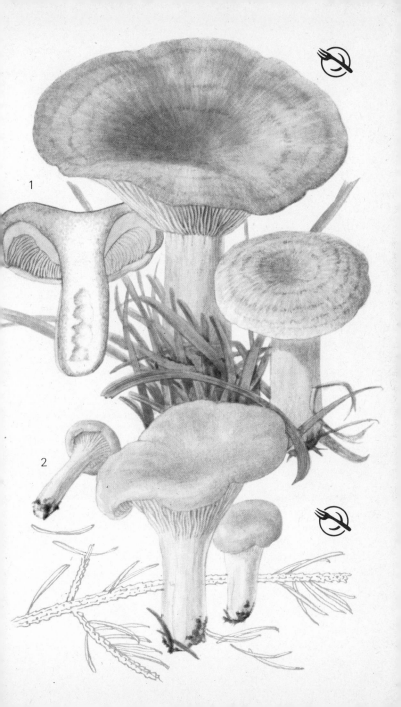

Lactarius volemus

Lactarius decipiens
Synonym: *Lactarius theiogalus*

Lactarius volemus is a pleasant and easily recognizable mushroom. It is particularly well distinguished by its plentiful supply of white milk, which has a mild taste, does not change colour and has a smell of pickled herrings (trimethylamin). When the fresh fruit-bodies are cut, the milk pours out in quantity, although this is less of a feature in dry, old fruit-bodies, which sometimes lack milk altogether. The conspicuous pickled herring smell grows stronger as the fruit-bodies die away.

Lactarius volemus is a good edible mushroom, which grows predominantly in well-established pine forests. It can be safely eaten even in its raw state, which is an unusual feature of mushrooms. Its caps are a delicacy when salted, spiced with carraway seeds and fried in hot fat. When preparing the mushroom in this way, the caps should be placed in the frying pan with the gills facing upwards. *Lactarius volemus* is also good for soups. It can, however, be mistaken for the very acrid *Lactarius rufus*, and it is wise to taste a small piece raw, in order to make sure that the flavour is mild.

Lactarius decipiens is one of the lesser known representatives of the *Lactarius* genus. It can be found in damp places in deciduous and coniferous forests and in some regions grows in large numbers. It can be distinguished from similar *Lactarius* species by its light-coloured cap and scarce white milk, which slowly turns yellow in the air. It has a bitter, resinous taste and is inedible.

1 Lactarius volemus:
Cap: 5–15 cm in diameter.
Stipe: 4–12 × 1–2 cm.
Occurrence: From summer to autumn.
Spores: 8–10 μm in diameter, colourless.

2 Lactarius decipiens:
Cap: 3–7 cm in diameter.
Stipe: 3–7 × 0.4–0.8 cm.
Occurrence: From summer to autumn.
Spores: 6–10 × 5–8 μm, colourless.

2

1

Lactarius piperatus
Synonym: *Lactarius pergamenus*

Lactarius vellereus

The impressive large white mushrooms, which can
be seen during summer in all types of forests,
usually belong to these two *Lactarius* species. Both
usually grow gregariously in groups or circles. In
shape they are similar and are rich in milk, which
flows freely from the flesh when bruised. This is
white, does not change colour and has an acrid
taste. The cap and stipe of *Lactarius vellereus* are soft
and velvety, whilst its gills are spread out. The cap
and stipe of *Lactarius piperatus* on the other hand are
smooth and its gills are crowded closely together.
It is inedible. This species is very similar to *Lactarius glaucescens*, whose milk is also initially white,
but turns greyish-green when exposed to the air.
This can be best observed on the bruised edges of
gills, to which the drops of milk cling that ultimately dry out in the form of tiny greyish-green
balls. Similar to this species is the pure white
Russula brevipes, which is distinguished by its lack
of milk and its mild taste. Its gills usually have
a pale blue-green circle at the point where they
are attached to the stipe. It is inedible. Although
Lactarius piperatus is acrid it can be prepared in
various ways if it is just boiled in water for
10 minutes, rinsed and drained. It can then be
seasoned and fried with bacon and onions.

*1   Lactarius
piperatus:*
Cap: 8–18 cm
in diameter.
Stipe:
4–8×2–3 cm.
Occurrence:
From summer
to autumn.
Spores:
8–9.5×5.5–7 μm,
colourless.

*2   Lactarius
vellereus:*
Cap: 10–20 cm
in diameter.
Stipe:
4–10×2–3 cm.
Occurrence:
From summer
to autumn.
Spores:
7.5–9.5×
6.5–8.5μm,
colourless.

Fly Agaric

Amanita muscaria

Amanita regalis

The Fly Agaric belongs to the childhood world of fairy tales. Apart from Boletus, it is the most popular mushroom. The red colour of its cap has always been taken as a poison warning, but, although the Fly Agaric is poisonous, its effects are not as dangerous as those of the Death Cap *(Amanita phalloides)* or the white *Amanita* species. The alkaloid called muscarine is the main component which causes poisoning if fresh or dry fruit-bodies of this mushroom are consumed in some quantity. The effect is rather similar to alcoholic intoxication, namely a disruption of the nervous and digestive systems. However, a healthy person usually gets over such poisoning quite quickly and without further after-effects.

This fungus grows in coniferous forests, especially those containing spruce and sometimes birch and with these it is often in symbiotic association.

Its closest relative is *Amanita regalis*, whose distinctive feature is a liver-like, yellowish-brown cap; it grows in mountainous spruce forests and is as poisonous as the Fly Agaric, containing the same muscarine alkaloid.

1   *Amanita muscaria:*
Cap: 5–15 cm in diameter.
Stipe: 10–25 × 1–3 cm.
Occurrence: From summer to autumn.
Spores: 10–12 × 7–10 μm, colourless.

2   *Amanita regalis:*
Cap: 5–12 cm in diameter.
Stipe: 8–16 × 1–2.5 cm.
Occurrence: Summer.
Spores: 9–10 × 6–9 μm, colourless.

Blusher
Amanita rubescens

Panther Cap
Amanita pantherina

It surprises some people to discover that there are some *Amanita* species that can be consumed without deleterious effects and that some of them are even very tasty mushrooms. This can be said of the Blusher, which grows in all types of forests. It is easily distinguished by its flesh, which turns pink especially at the base of the stipe, which is nearly always attacked by insect larvae. However, cases of mistaken identity leading to poisoning occur every year, for it is often confused with the Panther Cap. This species can be recognized by the different colour of its cap and the constant colour of its flesh. The shape of the widened base of the stipe is also different. While the Panther Cap has a low border near its base with the addition of 2—3 rings, the base of the Blusher is not bordered and is merely covered with several circles of protruberances. The true ring on the stipe of the Panther Cap is narrow, limp, smooth and without those longitudinal furrows that stand out clearly on the large membranous ring of the Blusher. The Blusher is an edible mushroom with an excellent flavour, especially when used for soups or for frying. It is unsuitable, however, for drying.

The Panther Cap regularly grows under oak trees and is very poisonous. It contain myco-atropine, which causes brain damage. The nature of the poisoning is very similar to that caused by an excessive consumption of alcohol.

1 Amanita rubescens:
Cap: 5–15 cm in diameter.
Stipe: 5–12 × 1–3.5 cm.
Occurrence: From summer to autumn.
Spores: 8–9 × 6–7 μm, colourless, amyloid.

2 Amanita pantherina:
Cap: 5–10 cm in diameter.
Stipe: 6–12 × 1–2 cm.
Occurrence: From summer to autumn.
Spores: 10–12 × 7–8 μm, colourless, nonamyloid.

Death Cap

Amanita phalloides

Amanita citrina
Synonym: *Amanita mappa*

The Death Cap is the most poisonous mushroom known to man. It grows in deciduous forests, especially under oak and hornbeam trees. Its cap is coloured in various shades of green and usually has additional grey or yellowish-brown patches, although in exceptional circumstances it can also be whitish or pure white. Its cuticle is streaked with radiating fibrils. It is either completely bare or occasionally has dried traces of its whitish veil. The gills are permanently white or whitish and this feature distinguishes it from champignons, whose gills are pink when young and later turn a dark brown or black. The base of the Death Cap's stipe widens out into a tall, membranous, whitish volva, whose upper edge has irregular lobes. The ring on the upper part of the stipe is fine, limp, white or whitish and has a smooth surface. Its white flesh has a mild, sweet, delicate taste and thus great care must be taken when picking Field mushrooms, because the Death Cap sometimes occurs in a pure white form.

Amanita citrina can easily be identified by its lemon or greenish-yellow cap, which is covered with numerous remains of the veil. Its basal bulb is large but without the membranous volva. Its flesh smells of raw potatoes, is not poisonous, but certainly cannot be recommended for consumption because of its unpleasant taste and the possibility of confusing it with the Death Cap.

1 *Amanita
phalloides:*
Cap: 5–12 cm
in diameter.
Stipe:
5–12 × 1–2 cm.
Occurrence:
VII—IX.
Spores:
8–10 × 7–9 μm,
colourless.

2 *Amanita
citrina:*
Cap: 3–10 cm
in diameter.
Stipe:
3–10 × 0.8–1.5 cm.
Occurrence:
From summer
to autumn.
Spores: 8–10 μm
in diameter,
colourless.

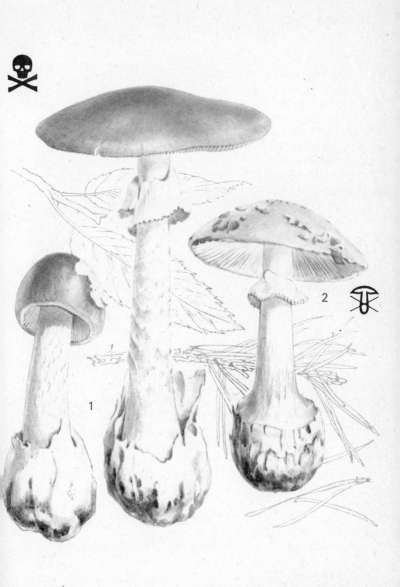

Amanita spissa
Amanita porphyria

As in the case of the Blusher *(Amanita rubescens)*, *Amanita spissa* is one of the most common of this genus. It grows in spruce and pine forests and can easily be recognized by its greyish cap, which is covered with white or greyish warts, although occasionally it is almost smooth. Its ring is longitudinally striated; the basal bulb of the stipe narrows downwards like an inverted cone. The stipe is either smooth or has rings of wart-like patches. Its white flesh does not change colour and smells of raw potatoes or beetroot. It is not poisonous but best avoided as it can so easily be confused with dangerous species.

Amanita porphyria is a poisonous species and is not very common. Its cap is almost smooth, grey in colour, but with a characteristic slightly purple tinge. Its stipe is similarly coloured, has a ring and a large basal bulb, which is similar in shape to that of *Amanita citrina*. Its limp ring is not striated. Like the Fly Agaric, it contains the alkaloid muscarine and so the symptoms and the course of poisoning by it are similar. It grows in coniferous forests.

1 Amanita spissa:
Cap: 5–12 cm in diameter.
Stipe: 5–10 × 1–3 cm.
Occurrence: From summer to autumn.
Spores: 9–10 × 7–8 μm, colourless.

2 Amanita porphyria:
Cap: 4–8 cm in diameter.
Stipe: 4–10 × 1–1.5 cm.
Occurrence: From summer to autumn.
Spores: 8–10 μm in diameter, colourless.

Grisette

Amanita vaginata
Synonym: *Amanitopsis vaginata*

Amanita umbrinolutea

The Grisette is a relatively slender, tall, very fragile mushroom with striated, thinly fleshed cap. Its gills are very dense and the basal volva is large and has lobed margins. It grows in damp places in coniferous forests. The stipe always lacks a ring and it was therefore formerly classified as a member of the independent *Amanitopsis* genus. The colour of its cap is changeable, but a typical Grisette has a grey cap on a whitish stipe and volva. The fruit-bodies with an orange or orange-brown or sometimes a slightly olive tinged cap are classified as *Amanita crocea*. Their stipes are similarly coloured and are characterized by transverse broken lines. The reddish-brown *Amanita umbrinolutea* can also be frequently seen. It has a dirty-whitish volva, and its stipe has also transverse irregular stripes.

All the above-mentioned *Amanita* species are edible; some mushroom-pickers even consider them tasty. Their disadvantage lies in their fragility and therefore they do not transport very well. Finally it is worth noting once again that, when such *Amanita* species are being gathered, constant vigilance must be exercised to avoid confusing them with the Death Cap *(Amanita phalloides)*, which has a similarly tall volva at the stipe's base; however, the Grisette is always without the characteristic ring.

1 Amanita vaginata:
Cap: 3–10 cm
in diameter.
Stipe:
7–15 × 0.8–1.5 cm.
Occurrence:
From summer
to autumn.
Spores: 9–12 μm
in diameter,
colourless.

2 Amanita umbrinolutea:
Cap: 6–12 cm
in diameter.
Stipe:
7–15 × 0.8–1.5 cm.
Occurrence:
From summer
to autumn.
Spores:
8–12 μm
in diameter,
colourless,
nonamyloid.

Blewits

Lepista saeva
Synonyms: *Tricholoma saevum, Tricholoma
bicolor, Tricholoma personatum*

Edible mushrooms can be found not only in forests,
but also in meadows, pastures and on grassy slopes.
Blewits are among the most substantial and tasty.
They even attract the inexperienced eye because
they often grow in circles in patches of dark green
grass, which are a strikingly deeper green than the
rest of the sward. A similar phenomenon may be
observed in the Fairy-ring champignon *(Marasmius
oreades)* and is due to the production of nitrogen,
which enriches the soil and provides additional
nourishment for green plants. This is one example
of the symbiosis of certain fungus mycelia and
adjacent green plants. The flesh of the Blewits has
a pleasant mushroom taste and scent, the stipe is
short and looks as if it had been stained with ink.

Blewits are excellent edible mushrooms, and can
be prepared in a number of ways. Their utility is
further increased by the fact that they can still
embellish our diet when other edible mushrooms
are on the decline. Even its frost-bitten specimens
can be found after the first frosts and can still be
used for cooking. They are suitable for soups, frying
in breadcrumbs and pickling in vinegar. According
to some authors the raw fruit-bodies contain a
substance that can cause the wastage of red blood
cells, but this substance is destroyed by boiling.
In some respects they are similar to Wood Blewits
(Lepista nuda), but differ in their gills, which are
never purple.

Cap: 7–15 cm
in diameter.
Stipe:
5–10 × 1–3 cm.
Occurrence:
IX–XI.
Spores:
6–8 × 4–5 μm,
pale pink.
Spore powder
pale pinkish.

Wood Blewits

Tricholomataceae

Lepista nuda
Synonyms: *Tricholoma nudum,*
Rhodopaxillus nudus

Wood Blewits are the twin fungi of Blewits *(Lepista saeva)*. They grow in woods, orchards, parks and along tree-lined lanes. In contrast to Blewits, the whole fruit-body is a beautiful amethyst purple when young. This colouring disappears with age and changes into cloudy purple or beige-brown, which is a feature of both the caps and gills. The flesh also later becomes whitish or greyish and has a pleasant scent. This characteristic purple colour, however, lasts for a long time on the stipe.

Cap: 6–15 cm in diameter.
Stipe: 5–10 × 1–2.5 cm.
Occurrence: IX–XII.
Spores: 6–8 × 4–5 μm, pale pink. Spore powder pale pinkish.

Wood Blewits are excellent edible mushrooms, appropriate for a variety of dishes. They are especially delicious when pickled in vinegar. They can be easily found by mushroom-pickers because they usually grow gregariously and also in the season when other edible mushrooms are scarce. Like Blewits, fresh fruit-bodies of Wood Blewits contain a substance which damages red blood-cells. However, it is neutralized by boiling and so thoroughly cooked mushrooms are not dangerous. Wood Blewits can be confused with some purple species of the *Cortinarius* genus. However, all of these are distinguished by their rust-brown spore powder, by the presence of the cobweb-like veil (cortina) and by their unpleasant smell.

Sulphur tuft

Hypholoma fasciculare

Hypholoma sublateritium

In summer and autumn the yellow fruit-bodies of the *Hypholoma* species can often be seen growing in large clusters on old tree stumps. The cap margins of young specimens are connected with the stipe by a cobweb-like whitish veil, which later almost disappears. Both the illustrated species look very much alike, but they can be easily distinguished by the colour of the flesh and by their taste. The flesh of the Sulphur tuft is a bright yellow and has a repulsive bitter taste, whilst that of *Hypholoma sublateritium* is a dirty white with a rust-coloured tinge at the base of the stipe and it has only a slight bitter taste. The former species has sulphur-yellow, later greenish gills, while in the latter species the gills are pale yellow, later turning to an olive-brown. When the mushrooms mature the gills of both species turn purple-black or chocolate-brown as a result of the colour of the ripe spores. *Hypholoma sublateritium* is sturdier with the cap a deeper black and the stipe not as vivid a sulphur-yellow, but rather more whitish in colour.

Sulphur tuft is poisonous but the strength of its poison varies according to the geographical location of its habitat. For example in Japan it is rated as one of the most poisonous mushrooms and judging by the number of poisonings, it ranks second only to the Death Cap *(Amanita phalloides)*. In Europe it has a weaker poison and accidents stemming from it are much rarer.

Hypholoma sublateritium, on the other hand, is not poisonous, but it is still inadvisable to pick it, because of the possible confusion with Sulphur tuft.

1   *Hypholoma fasciculare:*
Cap: 3–6 cm in diameter.
Stipe: 3–10×0.5–1 cm.
Occurrence: From spring to autumn.
Spores: 6–8×4–5μm, dirty yellow-brown.

2   *Hypholoma sublateritium:*
Cap: 5–8 cm in diameter.
Stipe: 5–12×0.5–1.5 cm.
Occurrence: From summer to autumn.
Spores: 6–8×3–4μm, dirty yellow-brown.

128

Clitocybe nebularis is one of the sturdiest representatives of its genus. It is readily identified by its cloudy whitish cap, whose surface has a slight ashgrey bloom, and by its sharp aromatic distinctive smell, reminiscent of soap. It grows gregariously in all types of woods and even outside them. *Clitocybe nebularis* is edible but of a poor quality, though some mushroom-pickers collect it and add it to a mixture of other mushrooms or pickle it in vinegar. It is advisable to scald the sliced mushrooms before proceeding further, otherwise they can cause indigestion.

Clitocybe clavipes is similar in shape to *Clitocybe nebularis*, but is smaller and the shades of brown, black or olive-green which characterize the cap also lack the distinctive bloom. Its stipe is very spongy and club-shaped near the base. Its mycelium becomes firmly embedded in needles, moss and leaves, so that when the fruit-body is pulled out, a part of this base comes out with the stipe. The fruit-body smells faintly of bitter almonds. This species usually grows singly in coniferous forests or mixed woods of pine and oak, but most often in the moss under larch trees. It is edible and particularly suitable for making soups.

1   *Clitocybe nebularis:*
Cap: 5–15 cm in diameter.
Stipe: 4–12 × 1.5–3 cm.
Occurrence: VIII–XI.
Spores: 6–8 × 3–4 μm, colourless.

2   *Clitocybe clavipes:*
Cap: 3–7 cm in diameter.
Stipe: 4–7 × 0.8–2 cm.
Occurrence: From summer to autumn.
Spores: 5–6 × 3–4 μm, colourless.

1

2

The coloration of *Clitocybe odora* differs from other members of this genus, in which the prevailing colours are white, whitish-grey, greyish-brown and brown. Instead, it has a copper, blue-green to green-grey cap with a whitish or greenish tinge on the gills and stipe. These features, along with the pleasant sweet aniseed scent of the whole fruit-body, distinguish it sufficiently from any other species. Its scent can be compared to that of fennel and is also shared by two other members of this genus, *Clitocybe suaveolens* and *Clitocybe fragrans*, although both of these have a completely different colouring: their caps are pale grey to ochre-brown in damp conditions and white in dry weather.

In calm weather conditions it is possible to smell the scent of *Clitocybe odora* at a distance of several metres away, especially when several specimens are growing together in one spot. This species is edible and best utilized when added to mixtures of other, less aromatic mushrooms. It grows predominantly in spruce forests amongst rotting needles. It loses its typical scent when it is dried out.

Cap: 3–10 cm in diameter.
Stipe: 3–8×0.6–1.2 cm.
Occurrence: Autumn.
Spores: 6–7×3–4μm, colourless.

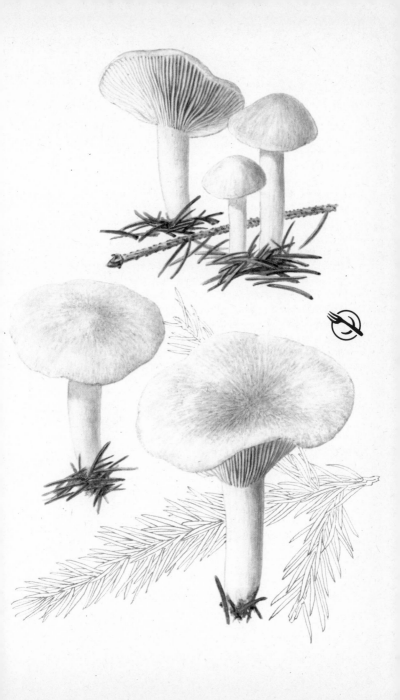

Clitocybe inversa is distinguished in colour from other related species by its orange-yellow, yellowish-red to leathery yellow cap. Its gills and stipe are similarly coloured and the flesh has a faint mushroom odour. The huge mycelium at the base of the stipe is white and grows deep down through the soil especially if this is composed of rotting pine needles. This mushroom grows gregariously in the humus of spruce forests, where it is sometimes distributed in large colonies or clusters or sometimes circles. It is edible, and particularly the caps of young fruit-bodies are picked and used for soups, sauces and for frying, although it is best mixed with other meaty mushrooms as the flesh of older specimens is relatively tough. Therefore, it is best suited for pickling in vinegar, which also disguises its slightly bitter and acidic flavour. It can also be dried and blended in mixtures with other mushrooms.

Clitocybe inversa is similar to *Clitocybe gilva*, which differs from the former in its lighter yellowish-brown to light brownish-ochre cap with numerous shallow, circular, spongy dark patches reminiscent of fruit-stones. Its gills are also lighter and whitish in young specimens, turning yellowish later. It grows in deciduous and coniferous forests, is perfectly edible and tastes even better than *Clitocybe inversa*.

Cap: 4–10 cm in diameter.
Stipe: 3–7 × 1–1.5 cm.
Occurrence: VIII–X.
Spores: 3–5 μm in diameter, colourless.

Tricholomopsis rutilans
Synonym: *Tricholoma rutilans*

Megacollybia platyphylla
Synonyms: *Tricholomopsis platyphylla,*
Collybia platyphylla

Some wood species of the Tricholomataceae family, which were originally classified as members of the genera *Tricholoma* and *Collybia*, form today independent genera. *Tricholomopsis rutilans* is a very common species of this group and is found growing on old stumps of pine-trees. It is a tidy-looking mushroom with a yellow cap, which is covered with numerous fine, red scales that grow fainter and merge with the yellow colour of the base as the mushroom ages. Its very young fruit-bodies are purple to purple-red, whilst its gills and stipe are a golden yellow, although part of the stipe is a deep red. This is an edible mushroom, but of an inferior quality and so it is seldom collected.

Megacollybia platyphylla is a wood mushroom with broad gills and has only a few points in common with other *Megacollybia* species. It is characterized by a grey or greyish-brown cap, radially streaked with fibrils and later becoming coarsely mealy. It also has unusually broad, well spaced, whitish gills. If the fruit-body is carefully pulled out, its prominent white mycelial roots (1—3 mm thick), which penetrate the rotting wood of old tree stumps, are evident on the stipe's base.

1 *Tricholomopsis rutilans:*
Cap: 5–12 cm
in diameter.
Stipe:
6–12 × 0.8–2 cm.
Occurrence:
From summer
to autumn.
Spores:
6–7 × 4–5.5 μm,
colourless.

2 *Megacollybia platyphylla:*
Cap: 5–15 cm
in diameter.
Stipe:
5–12 × 1–2 cm.
Occurrence:
From summer
to autumn.
Spores:
7–8 × 6–7 μm,
colourless.

Tricholoma saponaceum

In terms of colouring *Tricholoma saponaceum* is one of the mushroom 'chameleons'. The cap's cuticle comes in shades of white, grey, brown, green, light olive-green or also a leathery yellow and reddish colour. All these shades have an inclination to turn red eventually. Its gills exhibit a similar characteristic; at first they are whitish, later becoming yellowish to greenish-yellow and with age finally turning grey. The old fruit-bodies are usually reddish-brown or at least have red patches. The identity of *Tricholoma saponaceum* (and some other differently coloured species) is revealed by the presence of a specific smell, which resembles that of ordinary household soap. However, this is less conspicuous in fresh or young fruit-bodies.

Tricholoma saponaceum can be found in all types of woods, but particularly in spruce forests, where it grows both singly or in colonies, in valleys as well as on mountain slopes. Its habitat is the temperate zone of the northern hemisphere. It is inedible, as, along with *Lepista nuda*, it contains a substance which decomposes red blood cells. Although this toxin is destroyed by cooking, *Tricholoma saponaceum* can still precipitate indigestion in sensitive people.

Cap: 4–8 cm in diameter.
Stipe: 3–7 × 1–2.5 cm.
Occurrence: VIII–XI.
Spores: 5–6 × 3.5–4 μm, colourless.

In the autumn *Tricholoma terreum* appears in colonies in places with calcareous soil where black pines grow. Its colour is grey or greyish-brown; it has a delicate texture and its cap is streaked with fibrils and scattered with fine scales. Initially its gills are white with uneven edges but later turn grey as does its smooth white stipe. The flesh has a slight smell of raw potatoes and is also similar in taste.

This *Tricholoma* is not dependent on the black pine, although it frequently grows underneath it. However, it can also be found under other trees. It is a good edible mushroom, which may be prepared in a number of ways and is particularly delicious in soups. An exceptionally valuable feature is that it can still be found late in the season, when other edible mushroom are decreasing in numbers. A disadvantage is the small size of its fruit-bodies and the fragility of their flesh, which proves an obstacle in their transportation.

Some mushroom-pickers confuse *Tricholoma terreum* with *Tricholoma portentosum*, which is a sturdier and fleshier specimen; it has a smooth, radially fibrous cap and smells strongly of flour. Finally the confusion of the above species with the poisonous *Tricholoma pardalotum (T. tigrinum)* is unlikely, as this is a rare *Tricholoma* species, which has a sturdy body with a convex, scaly cap measuring up to 12 cm in diameter and with a stipe which turns brick red when bruised.

Cap: 3–8 cm in diameter.
Stipe: 3–6×0.8–1.5 cm.
Occurrence: IX–XI.
Spores: 5–7×4–5μm, colourless.

In terms of utility, two species of this genus are equally important. These are *Tricholoma portentosum* and *T. flavovirens (T. equestre)*, which are both excellent edible and delicious mushrooms. *Tricholoma portentosum* is a fleshy species with a greyish to greyish-black cap with black, sometimes purple-black fibrils on a white base. It is a little slimy in damp weather, has no scales and its margins are often irregularly lobed. The stipe and gills are white, with a prominent lemon-yellow tinge. The flesh has a pleasant floury scent and flavour. *Tricholoma flavovirens*, on the other hand, has a brownish-green to brownish-yellow cap, whilst its flesh has the pleasant smell of freshly milled flour. Care must be taken to avoid confusing it with the Death Cap.

Both *Tricholoma* species grow late into the autumn in large numbers in coniferous, especially pine, forests on a sandy soil. They have a multitude of uses, being good for sauces and soups, for pickling in vinegar and salt and also for drying. *Tricholoma portentosum* fried in breadcrumbs has a sweet taste and is a particularly attractive dish.

Tricholoma portentosum is sometimes confused with *Tricholoma argyraceum*, which is also edible but of an inferior quality. It can be distinguished by its fibrous cap and the yellowing tendency of its gills and stipe. It is, however, similar in smell and also grows prolifically in late autumn in coniferous forests, especially at the edges of spruce forests.

Cap: 3–10 cm in diameter.
Stipe: 4–8 × 1–2 cm.
Occurrence: Late autumn (IX–XII).
Spores: 5–6 × 3.5–5 μm, colourless.

Horse mushroom

Agaricus arvensis
Synonym: *Psalliota arvensis*

Yellow stainer

Agaricus xanthodermus
Synonym: *Psalliota xanthoderma*

Field mushroom

Agaricus campestris
Synonym: *Psalliota campestris*

This plate illustrates the three most common members of the Agaricaceae family. The Horse mushroom can be found in spruce forests and in open fields and is easily identified by its pure white fruit-body, which becomes a vivid yellow when bruised or scratched, and when cut, gives off a pleasant aniseed smell. Unlike other species of this genus its gills are never pink but greyish. The Yellow stainer is a similar mushroom but grows in warmer regions. It can be easily recognized by its vivid yellow flesh near the base of its stipe and by its unpleasant phenol (carbolic) smell, which is particularly evident during cooking. This species is best left alone because it can cause indigestion.

The Field mushroom is usually picked in pastures, meadows and fields. Its gills are a vivid pink at first, turning to a fleshy red and even a chocolate brown to black later. Unlike the others its flesh does not turn yellow when bruised.

The Field and Horse mushrooms are edible and popular mushrooms of the first quality. Momentary carelessness can sometimes lead to their confusion with the very poisonous *Amanita phalloides* ssp. *verna* and the Destroying Angel *(Amanita virosa)* or even with some white forms of the Death Cap *(A. phalloides)*. However, all these dangerous species have permanently white gills and a large volva at the base of the stipe.

1 Agaricus arvensis:
Cap: 6–15 cm in diameter.
Stipe: 6–12 × 1–2 cm.
Occurrence: From summer to autumn.
Spores: 6.5–8 × 4–5 μm, brown.

2 Agaricus xanthodermus:
Cap: 5–15 cm in diameter.
Stipe: 6–12 × 1–2 cm.
Occurrence: From summer to autumn.
Spores: 6–7 × 4–5.5 μm, brown.

3 Agaricus campestris:
Cap: 5–12 cm in diameter.
Stipe: 3–8 × 1–2 cm.
Occurrence: From summer to autumn.
Spores: 6.5–8 × 4–5 μm, brown.

Oyster fungus
Pleurotus ostreatus

Pleurotaceae

Flammulina velutipes
Synonym: *Collybia velutipes*

Tricholomataceae

Pleurotus ostreatus and *Flammulina velutipes* belong to those mushrooms species which prefer cold conditions and therefore form their fruit-bodies in the low temperatures of late autumn, in winter and early in spring. *Flammulina velutipes* is a true winter mushroom, which, during mild winters, can be found on tree stumps and at the base of trunks of numerous deciduous and occasionally coniferous tree species. Its fruit-bodies form rich clusters in parks, lanes and orchards. It can be easily recognized by the velvety surface of its stipe, which is a dark brown to blackish-brown at the base, and by its yellow cap, which becomes slimy in damp conditions. It has only a faint mushroom scent but cannot be mistaken for other gill fungi, because these usually do not grow at this time of the year. It is a good edible species, which adds a rich flavour to a variety of dishes. It is especially good for soups and for pickling in vinegar.

The Oyster fungus is found in several colour varieties and usually grows in tufts near the stumps and trunks of deciduous trees. Ash-grey or blue-grey caps are the most common. It is a very good edible mushroom and its caps fried in fat are delicious and taste something like fish. In recent years the Oyster fungus has been grown commercially in large quantities on the trunks of poplar trees and in a variety of timber.

1 Pleurotus ostreatus:
Cap: 5–20 cm in diameter.
Stipe: 2–5 × 1–2 cm.
Occurrence: From autumn through mild winters until spring.
Spores: 8–13 × 3–4 μm, colourless.

2 Flammulina velutipes:
Cap: 2–6 cm in diameter.
Stipe: 3–8 × 3–6 cm.
Occurrence: X–IV.
Spores: 7–9 × 4.5–6 μm, colourless.

Hygrophorus hypothejus

Synonyms: *Limacium hypothejum,*
Limacium vitellum

Hygrophorus lucorum

Synonym: *Limacium lucorum*

Both illustrated species are typical representatives
of late-autumn mushrooms. They are dependent
on certain species of trees: *Hygrophorus hypothejus*
predominantly on pine and *Hygrophorus lucorum* on
larch trees. After the first autumn frosts, the former
species grows gregariously in pine forests but only
if the preceding period has had favourably damp
weather. The olive to coffee brown, slimy cap
contrasts sharply with its egg-yolk yellow gills and
similarly coloured stipe. The stipe too is generally
slimy and has a prominent gelatinous ring, which
is the only remnant of its original slimy veil. The
flesh has a faint mushroom taste and scent.

Almost the whole fruit-body of *Hygrophorus
lucorum* is a lemon yellow. Like *Hygrophorus hypothejus,* this mushroom is also slimy on the cap and
stipe and has a pleasant mushroom scent. It
appears a little earlier than *H. hypothejus* and lasts
until the first frost. Both species are edible and
tasty, especially when used for soups and sauces.
Their value is increased by the fact that they grow
in a season which is otherwise poor in edible
mushrooms.

*1   Hygrophorus
hypothejus:*
Cap: 2–5 cm
in diameter.
Stipe:
3–8 × 0.1–0.3 cm.
Occurrence:
X–XII.
Spores:
7–8 × 4–5 μm,
colourless.

*2   Hygrophorus
lucorum:*
Cap: 2–6 cm
in diameter.
Stipe:
3–7 × 0.5–1 cm.
Occurrence:
X–XI.
Spores:
7–10 × 4–6 μm,
colourless.

Hygrophorus conicus

Synonym: *Hygrocybe conica*

The *Hygrophorus* genus includes white-spore gill mushrooms of medium or small size and of different coloration, with radial or lobed and attached gills. The gills are relatively supple and often quite broad and well spaced out.

Hygrophorus conicus, like the majority of mushrooms belonging to this species, is distinguished by its vivid colouring. Its sharply conical cap, slimy in damp weather, is a vivid yellowish-red; its gills are a pale yellow and the stipe blackens from the base upwards when bruised. The whole fruit-body turns black if the mushroom is dried up. The flesh is without any characteristic smell and tastes bitter. *Hygrophorus conicus* frequently grows outside the forest area, especially in grass along the roadside, on grassy slopes, meadows, pastures and on lawns. In the past it used to be considered poisonous, but this has proved to be inaccurate. However, it is best avoided because its taste is unpleasant, its fruit-bodies turn quickly black and so are not particularly attractive. It has an interesting and impressive colouring and can often be found in the company of other *Hygrophorus* species growing in grassy areas after rainfall.

Cap: 3–7 cm in diameter.
Stipe: 6–10 × 0.5–1 cm
Occurrence: From summer to autumn.
Spores: 9–10 × 5–6 μm, colourless.

Laccaria laccata
Laccaria amethystea
Synonym: *Laccaria amethystina*

The *Laccaria* genus is distinguished from the *Clitocybe* genus by its thick, well-spaced gills, which are densely covered with spore powder and flesh-pink or purple in colour. Its spore powder accumulated on a sheet of paper is, however, white despite the colour of the gills. These spores are rounded or broadly elliptical with a prominent spring network.

Both *Laccaria laccata* and *L. amethystea* are very abundant, common mushrooms in the damp forests of temperate zones. This is especially true of the former species. The difference between them is noticeable at first sight, although *Laccaria laccata* varies considerably in size and in the surface of its cap and stipe. Some varieties are now being considered as independent species, such as the sturdy *Laccaria proxima*, with the cap often completely covered with small scales and the stipe with rough longitudinal fibres. *Laccaria amethystea* cannot be confused with any other mushroom. Its young fruit-bodies are most attractive, being all deep purple. However, when old and dry the fruit-bodies turn pale and become whitish. Both species are edible but rarely gathered, because they are too colourful and too small.

1 *Laccaria laccata:*
Cap: 2–5 cm in diameter.
Stipe: 5–10 × 0.3–0.8 cm.
Spores: 7–10 μm in diameter, colourless.

2 *Laccaria amethystea:*
Cap: 2–5 cm in diameter.
Stipe: 5–10 × 0.3–0.8 cm.
Spores: 8–10 μm in diameter, colourless.
Occurrence: Both species from summer to autumn.

Fairy-ring champignon

Marasmius oreades

Collybia dryophila

The Fairy-ring champignon has been well known to country dwellers for a long time. Apart from the Boletus and the Chanterelle *(Cantharellus cibarius)* this used to be the only mushroom picked for eating. Its distinguishing characteristics are a pleasant smell of burnt almonds, an elastic yet firm stipe and its permanently white, sparse and deeply cut gills. It grows in circles in strips of dark green grass on the margins of forests, in pastures on downs and lawns, and alongside meadow paths. It is a tasty, popular mushroom, particularly good for preparing soups.

Collybia dryophila is a common mushroom of oak woods as well as pure coniferous forests. It is one of the best-known and also commonest representatives of its genus. It can be found in all types of forests, in valleys or in mountainous regions, where it associates with groups of low bushes often high above the tree line. It grows in an acidic or calcareous soil and is the commonest mushroom found in peat-bogs. *Collybia dryophila* is easily recognized but has a number of unusual varieties which are mainly to be found in deciduous forests. These have sulphur-yellow gills and are now considered as an independent species *(Collybia exsculpa)*.

Collybia dryophila is an edible species and again particularly good for soups. However, only its caps are collected as the stipes are too tough. It can be easily recognized by its conspicuously crowded gills, which are usually white, and by its pleasant mushroom taste and scent.

1 *Marasmius oreades:*
Cap: 3–5 cm
in diameter.
Stipe:
5–8 × 0.2–0.5 cm.
Occurrence:
From spring
to autumn.
Spores:
7–9 × 4–5 μm,
colourless.

2 *Collybia dryophila:*
Cap: 2–5 cm
in diameter.
Stipe:
3–6 × 0.3–0.5 cm.
Occurrence:
From spring
to autumn.
Spores:
4–5 × 2–3 μm,
colourless.

The *Mycena* genus includes mainly small, slender, fragile mushrooms with a thin stipe, a conical and membranous cap and white spore dust. Their colouring is variable and they can be found growing in a number of places, i.e. forests, on tree stumps, amongst the rotting remnants of plants and even on the margins of forests in grass and moss.

Mycena galericulata is immediately distinguished by the colour of its gills, which when mature almost always have a pink tinge. The spore powder of all *Mycena* species, however, is a pure white. The long, tough stipe often roots deep into the decaying wood of tree stumps. This fungus usually grows gregariously on the stumps and trunks of deciduous trees in low-lying areas and only rarely grows on conifers. It is an edible species, yet of lesser importance because of its small size. Only its caps are collected because the stipes are tough; the taste is reminiscent of cucumber.

Mycena polygramma is similar in appearance but is usually smaller, with an impressive blue-grey to silver-grey stipe, which has long roots and is longitudinally marked with thin lines. Its flesh is tasteless though edible. However, it is relatively unimportant because of its small size. Like *Mycena galericulata* it grows on the stumps of trunks of deciduous trees, either individually or in clusters.

1 *Mycena
galericulata:*
Cap: 2–6 cm
in diameter.
Stipe:
5–12 × 0.3–0.8 cm.
Occurrence:
From spring
to winter.
Spores:
8–13 × 6–8 μm,
colourless.

2 *Mycena
polygramma:*
Cap: 2–4 cm
in diameter.
Stipe:
3–10 × 0.3–0.5 cm.
Occurrence:
From summer
to autumn.
Spores:
8–12 × 6–8 μm,
colourless.

Some *Mycena* species can be recognized by their smell and one of these is *Mycena pura*, which smells strongly of radishes. The size and colouring of this species varies tremendously. The most typical variety has a light purple to pink-purple cap, but can also be seen with a bluish tinge, brown or white. The colour intensity changes when the mushroom dries out and is always lighter when moist. The tubular stipe is fragile, with a white woolly base. The sparse, deeply cut gills, which are sharply lobed near the stipe, are transversely furrowed and pale purple in colour.

Mycena pura can be found in all types of woods. Individual specimens or colonies grow in humus or organic waste, in rotting leaves and needles in damp places. In the past it was considered edible, but recently it has been proved to be poisonous. Such poisoning, which occurs after consuming it in large quantities, follows a similar pattern to that caused by the Fly Agaric, also this mushroom probably contains a toxic alkaloid muscarine. Fortunately, it can be easily distinguished from other purple edible gill fungi.

Cap: 2–4 cm in diameter.
Stipe: 3–7 × 0.3–0.5 cm.
Occurrence: V–X.
Spores: 5–6 × 2.5–3 μm, colourless.

Pluteus cervinus is one of the most common red-spore mushrooms which grow on stumps and rotting wood. Its relatively large fruit-bodies have a light to dark grey or greyish-brown cap, surmounting a thin, white stipe which is longitudinally streaked with thin dark fibrils. The gills are prominent and stand free from the stipe. At first they are white but then turn to a pale pink and later a fleshy red, when their spores ripen. Their margins are not different in colour from the rest of the gills, as opposed to the closely related *Pluteus atromarginatus*, whose gill edges have black margins. While *Pluteus cervinus* prefers the wood of deciduous trees, especially the stumps of birch trees, hornbeams, oaks and beeches, *Pluteus atromarginatus* grows exclusively on the wood of coniferous trees, most often on pines and spruces. However, it is not as abundant as *Pluteus cervinus*. Both species are edible, but of inferior quality and little nutritional value. Their flesh is very delicate and absorbent, so that they are easily damaged when transported. Mushroom-pickers only occasionally collect *Pluteus* but it can be used in soups and in fried mushroom mixtures.

Cap: 5–12 cm in diameter.
Stipe: 6–12 × 0.8–1.5 cm.
Occurrence: V–X.
Spores: 8–9 × 5–6 μm, pale pink.
Spore powder pink.

Some *Stropharia* species resemble small Field
mushrooms; they have the same colour of spore
powder, which is brown or purple-black, and a veil
that leaves a ring on the stipe. The commonest is
Stropharia coronilla, which has a cap up to 6 cm in
diameter and is a yellowish-white to light ochre in
colour. Its gills are a chocolate brown and it has
a relatively short stipe and striated ring. After a fall
of rain it grows on dry lawns, in mixed woods, in
pastures, parks and along the edges of fields.
Stropharia aeruginosa is a strikingly coloured species;
it has a verdigris-green, later ochre-coloured cap,
which is covered with a slimy layer and in young
specimens is flecked with white scales. Its green to
green-blue stipe is also slimy, covered with white
scales and showing a collar-like ring at its apex.
The bluish-green flesh has an unusual smell reminiscent of beetroot, which, in conjunction with
its colouring and slimy cuticle, does not make it an
attractive find. As it has an unpleasant taste, it is
rarely collected for cooking, and formerly it was
considered poisonous or at least regarded with
some suspicion.

However, the bluish-green *Clitocybe odora* is
edible, and can be distinguished by the absence of
the veil, an aniseed scent and white spore powder.

Cap: 3–10 cm
in diameter.
Stipe:
4–8 × 0.3–0.6 cm.
Occurrence:
VIII–XI.
Spores:
7–8 × 4–5 μm,
black-brown.

Cortinarius is the largest genus of gill-fungi, but their identification is often difficult even for an expert. All the species have spore powder ranging in colour through various shades of rusty yellow to a rusty brown. Their fruit-bodies have a cobweb-like, gelatinous veil (cortina), which leaves marks on the stipe in the form of fibrils or ring-like stripes. A further characteristic is their specific smell, which resembles that of raw potatoes. The colouring of the gills changes as the mushrooms mature and develop their ripening spores. The illustrated *Cortinarius mucosus* is most abundant in pine forests. Another related species, *Cortinarius caeruleipes*, grows in spruce forests and has a light purple stipe. All these can be collected for eating, but their taste is unappealing, which is also true of most other species in this genus. There are only a few known poisonous *Cortinarius* species, but also the number of really good edible kinds is limited.

Cap: 5–12 cm in diameter.
Stipe: 6–15×1–2 cm.
Occurrence: VIII–X.
Spores: 12–14× 5.5–6.5μm, rusty brown.

This is a neat-looking species and easily recognized at first sight. Its relatively sturdy fruit-bodies have a brick-red or reddish, rusty brown cap, with yellow, later cinnamon brown gills and a brown, club-shaped stipe, decorated with vermilion red broken stripes, which are remnants of the cortina. Its flesh lacks any specific taste or smell.

Cortinarius armillatus is associated with the birch trees of mixed forests and grows in an acid soil. Its fruit-bodies sometimes grow in small groups on mossy cushions or between fallen rotting leaves and needles. This species is usually classified as edible, but like the majority of *Cortinarius*, it is rarely collected. Its characteristic feature is the red striping on its stipe; these preclude any possibility of confusing it with other mushrooms.

The same *Telamonia* subgenus contains a large number of species, which differ both in size and colour. The majority of them have a cap which has a deeper colour when moist than when dry and a stipe with obvious remains of the veil distinctive rings.

Cap: 4–10 cm in diameter.
Stipe: 7–15 × 1–3 cm.
Occurrence: VIII–X.
Spores: 10–12 × 5–6.5 µm, light rusty brown.

Cortinarius cinnamomeoluteus is a small species, yellow-brown or olive-brown in colour, with radial fibrils on the cap. Its gills are light yellow when young, but later turn to a rusty olive-brown. The slender and vivid yellow stipe has a thin covering of fibrils left over from the veil. The lemon yellow flesh smells slightly of beetroot. The colouring of this species varies greatly. In earlier and now dated mycological literature several species were not distinguished from one another but grouped together and listed under the name of *Dermocybe cinnamomea*.

Cortinarius cinnamomeoluteus is not a very important species, but is one of the commonest mushrooms in coniferous forests. It grows on an acid soil, close to woodland paths, on moors, near bilberry bushes and on mossy banks. It is inadvisable to pick it because there are some poisonous species in this group, such as *Cortinarius orellanus*. Some are noted for the dry, felt-like to velvety cuticle on their caps. The fruit-bodies of numerous species classified in this group cover a wide range of colour pigmentation, especially yellow and red, which influences the overall colouring. Some species are in fact a vivid red or orange. One of these is *Cortinarius cinnabarinus*.

Cap: 3–5 cm in diameter.
Stipe: 5–10 × 0,3–0.6 cm.
Occurrence: V–XI.
Spores: 7–9 × 5–6 μm, rusty yellow.

Large tufts of *Pholiota destruens* appear on willow and on felled poplar trees that have been left lying for some time on the ground. It also grows on stumps and sometimes directly on living trees. It is a very sturdy fungus with firm flesh and is one of the largest of its genus. Its dirty beige to light brown caps, which are slimy when moist, are scattered with white scales. The edges of the young caps are connected by a whitish veil with the stipe and later this is covered with irregularly shaped velar remnants. On the equally scaly stipe the veil leaves faint ring-like traces. The brownish gills have uneven, irregularly serrated edges. *Pholiota destruens* is inedible and its bitter, very tough flesh has a strong, unpleasant mushroom odour.

Another common member of this genus, *Pholiota squarrosa*, has already been described in the section on Honey fungus.

Cap: 5–20 cm in diameter.
Stipe: 5–16 × 1–3 cm.
Occurrence: VIII–XI.
Spores: 7.5–9 × 5–5.5 μm, rusty brown.

St. George's mushroom

Tricholomataceae

Calocybe gambosa
Synonyms: *Tricholoma gambosum,*
Calocybe georgii

Entoloma sinuatum

Entolomataceae

Synonyms: *Entoloma lividum,*
Rhodophyllus sinuatus

The appearance of the St. George's mushroom signifies the advent of spring. This fleshy mushroom with its pleasant shape is easily recognizable. Apart from other features it has narrow, densely crowded gills and a very strong floury taste and smell. In some regions it is very popular and much sought after. Mushroom-pickers look for it in grassy patches outside woods, on slopes, in meadows, by the sunny edges of woods and in orchards. Sometimes it hides in thick grassy clumps so that it can be easily overlooked. It can be found far outside the forest as well as close to trees and bushes, particularly deciduous ones. It is a very tasty and valuable mushroom as it grows in a season which produces few edible species. It can be prepared in a number of ways and is usually added to sauces and soups.

The very poisonous *Entoloma sinuatum* is similar in appearance to the St. George's mushroom. While the latter has a pure white spore powder, the former has a pale pink spore dust. This is responsible for the pink colouring of the gills, which also have an additional orange tinge. *Entoloma sinuatum* is a wood species of the warm regions (especially the south of France) and grows in summer and autumn, when the St. George's mushroom is only rarely to be found. It grows in a calcareous soil under oak, hornbeam and beech trees.

1   *Calocybe*
gambosa:
Cap: 5–12 cm
in diameter.
Stipe:
3–6×1–2.5 cm.
Occurrence:
IV–VI.
Spores:
4–7×2–4µm,
colourless.

2   *Entoloma*
sinuatum:
Cap: 5–20 cm
in diameter.
Stipe:
8–20×1–3 cm.
Occurrence:
VII–IX.
Spores:
8–10×7–9µm,
light pink.

Common Earth-ball

Scleroderma citrinum
Synonym: *Scleroderma aurantium*

Sclerodermataceae

Puff-ball

Lycoperdon perlatum
Synonym: *Lycoperdon gemmatum*

Lycoperdaceae

The fruit-bodies of the Common Earth-ball are sturdy and white when young, but later their entire inside changes to dark green spore powder, which is periodically released from the fruit-bodies through cracks in their exterior wall. This mushroom is very aromatic and gives off an intense, spicy smell. It can be found in all types of woods, but most frequently in pine woods with sandy subsoil. Similar in nature to the illustrated species is *Scleroderma verrucosum*, whose fruit-body narrows into a thick stipe, which terminates in the mycelium cluster. *Scleroderma* species are slightly poisonous, and best avoided.

1 *Scleroderma citrinum:*
Fruit-body:
3–10 cm
in diameter.
Occurrence:
From summer
to autumn.
Spores: 7–15 μm,
black-brown.

Various species of Puff-balls provide a striking feature in all types of forests. The illustrated *Lycoperdon perlatum* is the most common of them. It has prominent large, conical warts and thorns, which are easily detached from its surface and leave square hollows. All Puff-balls are edible when they are young and unripe, that is when they are still white inside. They are very tasty and give an excellent flavour to soups. The inside of the ripe fruit-body soon disintegrates into an olive-yellow to dark brown powder, which is in reality a mass of spores. These are finally ejected through a small aperture near the apex of the fruit-body.

2 *Lycoperdon perlatum:*
Fruit-body:
2–8 cm high
2–5 cm wide.
Occurrence:
From summer
to autumn.
Spores: 3.5–5 μm,
pale yellow.

GLOSSARY
OF MYCOLOGICAL TERMS

amyloid — the change of the spore walls or of the fungal filaments into various shades of blue, sometimes a slate grey or at other times a deep blue or bluish-green. This occurs in solutions containing iodine, particularly Melzer's reagent. The opposite is nonamyloid.

annulus — the ring or remnant of the veil on the surface of the stipe, which takes the form of a collar or a ring. It originally connected the edge of the cap with the stipe.

apothecium — the open cup- or saucer-like fruit-body of a Discomycete.

ascospore — a spore born through sexual reproduction in the sac (ascus).

ascus — sac-like or tubular body bearing spores internally in Ascomycetes.

basidiospore — a spore of Basidiomycetes, which is sexually reproduced in the basidium and separated from it at the end of a surface protrusion.

basidium — club-shaped or tubular, cellular body, bearing spores which have developed sexually and externally on protrusions; it is characteristic of Basidiomycetes.

cap — the widened part of the fruit-body, bearing on its underside the hymenophore.

chemical reagents — substances used in the preparation of a microscopic specimen for the softening or better delineation of the fungal tissue; or like Melzer's reagent (q.v.) also used for identification through colour staining. The colour reaction shown by the flesh of the fresh fruit-bodies can also be tested with the help of various other chemical reagents; the most common is an aqueous solution of green vitriol, phenol (carbolic acid), sulpho vanillin and benzidine.

conidium — an asexual, vegetative spore produced on a conidiophore or a fungal filament.

coprophagous — feeding on dung or manure.

cortina — the cobweb-like, partial veil between the cap margin and the surface of the upper part of the stipe.

detritus — a layer of decaying parts of dead plants lying on the soil's surface.

177

dextrinoid — when the spore mass turns yellow-brown or red-brown in Melzer's reagent (a synonymous term is pseudoamyloid).

eccentric — used in reference to a stipe which coalesces with the cap anywhere between the the centre and the edge of its underside.

fructification — the ability of fungi to produce fruit-bodies; also used to denote the growing period of fungi.

fruit-body — a part of the thallus containing the propagative organs and spores.

heterotrophic — organisms which do not contain a photosynthetic colouring agent and receive organic nourishment directly from green plants, their dead remnants or even from animal bodies.

hyphae — fungal filaments.

hygrophanous — in damp conditions a dark-coloured cap soaked with water changes and loses colour when it dries out.

hymenium — a pallisade-like structure, made up of the fertile layer of basidia in Basidiomycetes or of asci in Ascomycetes, where it is also known as the thecium (q.v.).

Melzer's reagent — a solution of chloral hydrate in water with the addition of potassium iodide and iodine (i.e. KJ 1.5 g, J 0.5 g, distilled water 20 cm³, chloral hydrate 22 g). This reagent was discovered and first used by the Czech mycologist V. Melzer. It is one of the most indispensable and frequently used reagents in the study of fungi and their identification.

mycelium — the vegetative portion of the thallus of a fungus which derives its nourishment from the substrate.

mycorrhiza — the symbiotic association of the mycelium with the roots of green plants.

oidia — a thin-walled propagative cell resulting from the disintegration of the vegetative thallus.

ornamentation — the multi-shaped protrusions growing on the external spore wall.

paraphysis — sterile filaments filling the space between the asci.

parasite — a parasitic fungus, one which gains nourishment from living organisms and therefore causes their decay or complete destruction.

perithecium — a flask-shaped fruit-body of the Pyrenomycetes (Pyrenomycetales), usually containing a small opening near the apical pore.

photosynthetic dye — a colouring agent with the help of which the plant is capable of assimilation (i.e. the production of organic substances, especially sugars), from which it builds up its body

178

from simple mineral substances (i.e. CO_2, H_2O), derived from the soil and solar radiation.

pseudoamyloid — see dextrinoid.

resupinate — lying flat on the substratum, especially in reference to the fruit-bodies of numerous Aphyllophorales.

saprophyte — living on dead organisms, their remnants and other organic substances.

sclerotium — a hard tuberous mass of closely packed hyphae; this is capable of producing fruit-bodies.

septum — a dividing transverse or longitudinal wall in the hyphae and spores.

sexual propagation of fungi — the process during which the plasmatic and nuclear content of two sexually differentiated cells is achieved and followed by the development of spores.

spore — the reproductive single or multicellular body, analogous to seeds in higher plants, but lacking the embryo.

substrate — the base on which a fungus lives and from which it usually draws its nutrients.

thecium — a pallisade-like structure composed of asci (in Discomycetes).

thallus — the fungal body.

trama — the loosely woven hyphal tissue forming the central substance of the lamellae or other projections of the hymenophore.

vegetative or asexual propagation of fungi — during this process the thallus disintegrates and specific cells are produced without an earlier fusion of two sexually differentiated cells taking place.

velum — the external membrane (veil) of the fruit-body; it is divided into the external and internal veil.

volva — a tall membranous sac around the base of the stipe, which is a remnant of the veil.

BIBLIOGRAPHY

Ainsworth, G. C. and Bisbey, G. R.: *Dictionary of Fungi*. Commonwealth Mycological Institute, Kew, Surrey, 1961.

Alexopoulos, C. J.: *Introductory Mycology*. John Wiley and Sons, 1963.

Bessey, E. A.: *Morphology and Taxonomy of Fungi*. The Blakiston Co., Philadelphia. Toronto, 1952.

Dennis, R. W. G.: *British Ascomycetes*. Lehre, 1968.

Dennis, R. W. G., Orton, P. D. and Hora, F. B.: *New check list of British Agarics and Boleti*. Trans. brit. mycol. Soc. Suppl., 1960.

Lange, J. E. and Lange, M.: *Collins Guide to Mushrooms and Toadstools*. W. M. Collins Sons & Co. Ltd. London, 1963.

Miller: *Mushrooms of North America*. Chanticleer Press Inc. New York.

Pearson A. A.: A series of Monographs on fungi obtainable from the Editor, The Naturalist, University of Leeds.
The Genus Russula.
The Genus Lactarius.
British Boleti.
The Genus Inocybe.
The Genus Mycena.

Ramsbottom, J.: *Mushrooms and Toadstools*. The New Naturalist. Collins, London, 1953.

Savonius, Moira: *The All Colour Book of Mushrooms and Fungi*. Octopus Books Ltd. London, 1973.

Singer, R.: *The Agaricales (Mushrooms) in Modern Taxonomy*. Lilloa. 2nd ed, 1961.

Periodicals:

Index of Fungi. Commonwealth Mycological Institute, Kew.

Transactions of the British Mycological Society, London. Cambridge University Press.

INDEX